For dear friends Sidney and Joann,
who've actually been to Syracuse.

al Back
Nov, 1998

Movie Palace Masterpiece

Saving Syracuse's Loew's State/Landmark Theatre

Alfred Balk, Editor

Landmark Heritage Series
Landmark Theatre Foundation Syracuse, N.Y.

Acknowledgements

Dedicated to the late Dr. Vernon F. Snow of the John Ben Snow Foundation and to the many volunteers who quietly and selflessly united to save the architectural treasure originally known as Loew's State, now the Landmark, Theatre, in Syracuse.

Grant to underwrite publication:
The John Ben Snow Foundation, Syracuse, N.Y.

Designer/Production Editor:
Ann G. Stoltie

Production assistance:
S.I. Newhouse School of Public Communications, Syracuse University

Research assistance:
Local History Department, Onondaga County Central Library

Copyrighted material:
Syracuse Newspapers' copyrighted material reprinted with permission. All rights reserved.

Other copyrighted material:
Onondaga Historical Association, Syracuse.
Theatre Historical Society of America, Elmhurst, Ill.
American Movie Classics Magazine, Boston, Mass.
The Best Remaining Seats, Ben M. Hall, Clarkson N. Potter, Inc., New York
American Picture Palaces, David Naylor, Van Nostrand Reinhold Co., New York.
Avery Architectural and Fine Arts Library, Columbia University.

Material from personal collections:
George Hawley, Samuel Kalin, Charles Marvin, Joseph Bangnoski

Balk, Alfred W., 1930-

Movie Palace Masterpiece: Saving Syracuse's Loew's State/Landmark Theatre
ISBN 0-8156-8123-2
Copyright c 1998 Landmark Theatre Foundation
Published in 1998 by The Landmark Theatre Foundation, 362 S. Salina Street, Syracuse, N.Y. 13202. All rights reserved. No part of the contents of this book may be reproduced without the written permission of the Publisher.

Distributed by Syracuse University Press, 1600 Jamesville Avenue, Syracuse, N.Y. 13244

Contents

Introduction

This book is about a world-class 1928 movie palace. But it is also about a remarkable heritage dating to Erie Canal days.

Jenny Lind, Sarah Bernhardt, and Charles Dickens all performed in Syracuse's ornate 19th-century theaters. It became a mainstream vaudeville and pre-Broadway "tryout" town. It spawned the Shubert theater dynasty and the man who founded *Variety*, Sime Silverman.

In movies, it midwifed the Biograph camera that made possible the Biograph Studios of Mary Pickford, Mack Sennett, and D.W. Griffith. A Syracusan, John Wall, helped two nearby Auburn, N.Y. wizards, Theodore Case and Earl Sponable, invent soundtrack "talkies." The Schine theater-chain family's first venture in nickelodeons occurred in Syracuse. In the Twenties its Salina St. was a "Little Broadway" of dazzling movie and stage-show marquees.

These attracted one principal in this book, moviehouse tycoon Marcus Loew, who created the Metro-Goldwyn-Mayer studios. He commissioned another principal, architect Thomas Lamb, to create the *piece de resistance* of some 300 moviehouses Lamb designed. It was Syracuse's Loew's State Theatre, now recorded in the National Register of Historic Places as "new 'fantasy' architecture...one of the finest examples [of that] popular for movie theaters of the 1920s and 1930s."

These pages document this treasure's--and its era's--saga, in photos (sixteen pages in color), reminiscences, and news reports courtesy of The Syracuse Newspapers. They also chronicle the compelling story of the theater's rescue from demolition and its new life, begun June 30, 1978, as the nonprofit, citizen-owned Landmark Theatre.

That chapter is yet to be concluded. Many thousands of dollars are required for restoration, from structural upgrading to replacement of the "mighty Wurlitzer" organ, removed in the Sixties. This will require massive support from foundations, businesses, government bodies, and individuals. We hope that this book might stimulate that, as well as renewed interest in historic preservation and in touring or attending an event at this magnificent movie palace masterpiece.

A.B.

Alfred Balk is a former editor at *Saturday Review*, *Columbia Journalism Review*, and *World Press Review* magazines; the author of several books and many magazine articles; and a former journalism professor at Columbia and Syracuse Universities. A member of the Landmark Theatre Foundation Board of Directors, he organized its archives, publication, and tours programs.

'Theatertown'

In the Roaring Twenties, Syracuse's Salina Street was a "Little Broadway" bespeaking an extraordinary entertainment heritage: posh 19th-century playhouses, pre-Broadway tryout productions, mainline vaudeville, and early movie ventures that included a demonstration by the cinema's founders, Louis and August Lumiere. By the mid-Twenties, its "Theater Row" on Salina included three moviehouses designed by master theater architect Thomas W. Lamb: the Temple (later Paramount) and the Strand and Keith's shown below.

Postcard reproductions courtesy George Hawley

'Founding Father' Loew

To the surprise of many, the name Marcus Loew was absent from "Theater Row." As excerpts from *Photoplay* (1927) illustrate, Loew was an entertainment legend. A son of Viennese immigrants, he had struggled upward from the fur business to nickelodeon promoter, theater-chain owner, and movie studio entrepreneur—most spectacularly, in 1924 when he merged his first studio acquisition, Metro Pictures, into a larger Metro-Goldwyn-Mayer.

Little Journeys *to*

The Homes of
Famous Film
Magnates

By Terry Ramsaye
Author of "A Million and One Nights"

The Fourth of a Remarkable Series
of First Hand Studies
of the Big Men of Screendom

Marcus Loew as he is today, the head of a hundred million dollars' worth of entertainment enterprises

Photoplay, August, 1927. Archives of Theatre Historical Society of America, Elmhurst, Ill.

A CERTAIN two men stepped into the lobby of the office building at 1540 Broadway one recent morning, and thence into a waiting elevator. One of these men was the jolly mixer type, tall and cheery and knowing everybody. His companion was an inch or two below the medium, slight, grey and most unobtrusive of dress and manner.

"Twelfth, Bill," said the tall one, with a nod to the elevator operator.

"Howdy," responded that uniformed factotum. "How's tricks?" He slammed the gates, flicked the signal panel clear and threw the starting lever. As the car shot upward he turned and addressed this tall man whom he knew as the occupant of an office above. "I been here two years and I ain't seen the big boy yet—I'd like to meet him just once —that guy Loew."

"Then just turn around, Bill."

The operator flushed, jammed his car and stood stuttering in confusion as he faced the little man before him. Marcus Loew grinned and stuck out his hand.

"Glad to meet you, Bill—come in and see me some day when you are not too busy."

Now it begins to look as though Bill and "that guy Loew" are going to be good friends. And that is the kind of a guy Marcus Loew is—inconspicuous, quiet, good natured, and easy to overlook in a crowd, meanwhile one of the most extraordinary of men and extraordinary in success. His interests include the Loew Theatrical Enterprises, with nearly four hundred theaters in the United States, some seventy-and-odd theaters in Europe and South Amer-

ica, and the Metro-Goldwyn picture producing and distributing concern with a world wide business. A total of more than eight thousand employees are marshalled in the Loew army. He says they work with him, not for him.

> About twenty-three years ago Loew started with peep show arcades in an endeavor to interest and please this Average Person a penny's worth at a time. Then Loew and the Public began to get acquainted and presently by steps of about five cents each the entertainment developed into the modern institution of the motion picture with an admission price in the vicinity of fifty cents. Meanwhile both Loew and his friend, the Public, have grown more prosperous, especially Loew, who has accumulated a fortune estimated at from thirty to forty millions.

> MARCUS LOEW'S business career began in his early boyhood when he graduated himself from the third grade of the public school. He rented the right to vend newspapers on the corner in front of Bill McGurk's saloon on the Bowery. It was a percentage contract with half a block protection on both sides. Young Marcus early decided to expand the business and sub-leased the corner to another boy. He took in other corners, by conquest and purchase and developed the chain idea.

> Young Mr. Loew became a newspaper publisher at the age of sixteen. He was a printer's devil on the East Side when the notion infected him. He persuaded the boss to let him launch the East Side Advertiser. Then Marcus forthwith traded advertising space for a suit of clothes and a derby hat. After that the lad became an office boy in a fur concern and in time a partner in a fur business.

Creative Genius Lamb

In 1921, Marcus Loew had tried and failed to buy Syracuse's Empire Theatre. Subsequently, he explored sites for a new downtown moviehouse and chose Thomas W. Lamb as architect. Among accolades accorded the Scottish-born Lamb, who had apprenticed as a New York City building inspector, was *Motion Picture News'* characterization as "pioneer and foremost" in his field.

Thomas White Lamb was born in 1871 in Dundee, Scotland, and crossed the Atlantic with his parents before he was a teenager. A family story relates that the Lambs arrived in Canada before settling in New York by 1883. Nothing is known of this Canadian interlude.[1]

Lamb's father's employment with a large engineering firm may have had some influence on his son's interest in constructing buildings. Thomas opened an architectural office as early as 1892 at the age of 21, apparently before he had embarked on a course of specialized training. He is recorded in the 1892 directory of the American Institute of Architects as "doing general work" and with an office at 487 5th Ave.[2]

In 1894 (at the age of 23) Lamb enrolled in the General Science Program at New York's Cooper Union for the Advancement of Science and Art. He, with all the other students at this private institution, had a full-tuition scholarship. Lamb graduated in 1898 with a Bachelor of Science degree, but not a degree in architecture or engineering. He took only two courses related to his career: mechanical drawings and acoustics.[3]

Lamb started a "job book" in this period, though only one project, Job No. 1, "St. Nicholas Skating Rink" at 66th Street and Columbus in Manhattan dates from 1895. (The drawings are identified with the names of Thomas Lamb, Ernest Flagg, and W.B. Chambers.) In the job book, jobs 2 and 3, "Sketch for Hospital" and "Apt. for E. Meyer" are undated. The roster did not begin in earnest until a decade had passed.

While maintaining his architectural practice and studying at Cooper Union, Lamb was working as a building inspector with the City of New York. He acknowledged later that he had worked at New York City's Bureau of Buildings for five years, first as an inspector and later as a plan examiner.[4]

His experience there was to serve him well, as he ". . . encountered a wide variety of building types and construction problems." He also encountered future moguls of movie theater empires like Marcus Loew and William Fox. These men were seeking permits as well as young architects who were open to designing their novel type of building. Lamb soon developed a theater specialty, based on "his ready knowledge of the building code and quick solutions to the nagging problems of sight lines, acoustics and structure [and crowd safety] posed by theaters . . ."[5]

An Architect's Progress: Thomas White Lamb
by Hilary Russell

Excerpt from Lamb's corporate promotion booklet (top) and contract for Loew's State (#2328), as registered in the Thomas Lamb, Inc. "Job Book" (bottom).

Hereunder is a partial list showing various types and locations of buildings for which, and some of the clients for whom Thomas W. Lamb, Inc. rendered the architectural services

Madison Square Garden, Eighth Avenue	New York City
Loew's Palace Theatre	Washington, D. C.
Greyhound Terminal, Fiftieth Street	New York City
Capitol Theatre, Broadway at 50th Street	New York City
Fox 16 story Office Building and Theatre	Philadelphia, Pa.
20 story Apartment Bldg., Madison Ave. and 96th St.	New York City
French Casino and Commercial Building	Miami, Florida
Paramount Hotel, West 46th Street	New York City
Metro Office Building and Theatre	Cairo, Egypt
International Casino, Broadway and 44th Street	New York City
Pantages Theatre, Yonge Street	Toronto, Canada
Kings County Hospital, O.P.D. Bldg.	Brooklyn, N. Y.
RKO Theatre and Office Bldg., East 86th Street	New York City
Pythian Temple, 71st Street and Broadway	New York City
Metro Theatre	Bombay, India
Loew's State Office Building, 45th Street and Broadway	New York City
Residence, Harry Crandall	Washington, D. C.
Loew's 103rd Street Theatre	Cleveland, Ohio
Pickwick Arms Hotel, East 51st Street	New York City
Loew's 175th Street Theatre	New York City
Fountain Square Hotel	Cincinnati, Ohio
Greyhound Terminal	Pittsburgh, Pa.
Trans Lux Theatre, Walnut Street	Philadelphia, Pa.
N.V.A. Hospital	Saranac, N. Y.
Loew's 72nd Street Theatre, East 72nd Street	New York City
Metro Theatre	Johannesburg, S. Africa
Famous Players Theatre	Vancouver, Canada
Loew's Office Building and Theatre	Ottawa, Canada
Fox Theatre, Market Street	San Francisco, Cal.
Empire Theatre	London, England
Greyhound Terminal	Detroit, Michigan
Metro Theatre	Adelaide, Australia
Trans Lux Theatre and N.B.C. Studio	Washington, D. C.
Tivoli Theatre	Washington, D. C.
Metro Theatre	Puerto Rico
Keith Theatre and Office Building	Syracuse, N. Y.
Metro Theatre	Durban, S. Africa

American Community Theatres	Loew's, Inc.
Bowery Savings Bank	Mutual Life Insurance Company
City Bank Farmers Trust Company	National Broadcasting Company
City of New York	New Madison Square Garden Corporation
Famous Players Canadian Corporation	Poli Circuit
Fox Theatres, Inc.	Radio Keith Orpheum Corporation
Greyhound Lines, Inc.	Trans Lux Movies Corporation

Avery Architectural and Fine Arts Library, Columbia University.

Breaking the News

Syracuse's first reports of the project surfaced in February, 1926, along with photos of a venerable hotel it would displace.

Syracuse Journal, Feb. 19, 1926

$2,000,000 THEATER TO REPLACE HOTEL

Three and a half million dollars figure in a realty deal whereby the Jefferson Hotel (above) was sold for $1,600,000 by Julius Goldman (right, below) to Marcus Loew (left, below). A $2,000,000 theater building will replace the hotel.

MARCUS LOEW CONCERN WILL ERECT THEATER

Purchase Price $1,600,000; New Building to Cost $2,000,000.

LARGEST IN CITY

Transaction Made Possible Through Efforts of Eagan Office.

Official confirmation of sale of the Jefferson Hotel property, owned by Julian Goldman, to the Marcus Loew theatrical concern, which plans immediate erection of a theater and office building, was made Friday by the Eagan Real Estate Co. News of the sale was published last week exclusively in The Journal.

Purchase price for the property was $1,600,000. Plans for the new building call for expenditure of a minimum of $2,000,000. All leases on the property expire May 1, and the New York company plans to start on that date razing the present building and pressing forward construction of the new 10-story structure.

Post-Standard, Feb. 20, 1926

HOTEL PROPERTY SOLD TO LOEWS

Theater Interests Announce Plan to Erect Playhouse and Office Building.

BREAK GROUND MAY 1

$2,000,000 Structure of 12 Stories to Replace the Jefferson.

Julian Goldman of New York has sold to Loews, Inc., the Jefferson hotel property at South Salina and Jefferson streets, which will be developed at once for theatrical and business purposes. The Loews own and operate theaters in 100 cities.

It is proposed to break ground May 1 for a theater and office building which will cost $2,000,000. The site brought $1,600,000. The property has a frontage of 127 feet in South Salina street and 194 feet in West Jefferson street. The Jefferson hotel, one of the landmarks of the city, was remodeled a short time before Mr. Goldman, who has a store in Syracuse, purchased the property.

The new theater will accommodate 3,000 persons and it is expected that the building will be ready for occupancy next year. Marcus Loew will direct the development. Mr. Loew negotiated five years ago for the purchase of the Gurney building, which contains the Empire theater, but the deal was not closed.

Since that time Mr. Loew personally and his various picture and vaudeville interests have watched developments in Syracuse. Negotiations for the property at South Salina and Jefferson streets was started a number of months ago. It is believed that Mr. Loew will combine pictures and vaudeville as the attractions in the new theater.

The building is to be 12 stories high, the first six stories accommodating the theater, and the balance being used for offices. There will be stores in Salina and Jefferson streets, some of which will open into the broad entrance to the theater. Leases expire May 1 which makes it possible to start the new building without delay. L. T. & Edward Eagan

7

Blueprinting a Masterpiece

Given virtually a blank check by Loew, Lamb designed the city's largest and grandest movie palace, a meld of Hindu, Persian, and Oriental influences. Its 2,900-seat auditorium, with a sweeping curvelinear balcony, matched the height of the building's eight-story office wing. Its four-story, L-shaped lobby was framed by an overhead "Musicians Gallery," elephantine mural, massive mirrors, carved plaster pillars, diverse enclaves for lighting, and a "Grand Staircase" ascending in chandelier-lit splendor to the mezzanine "Grand Promenade." Heightening the opulence would be furnishings from two mansions, one that of the legendary Commodore Vanderbilt in Manhattan.

Samples (reduced) of Lamb construction drawings. *Landmark Theatre Archive.*

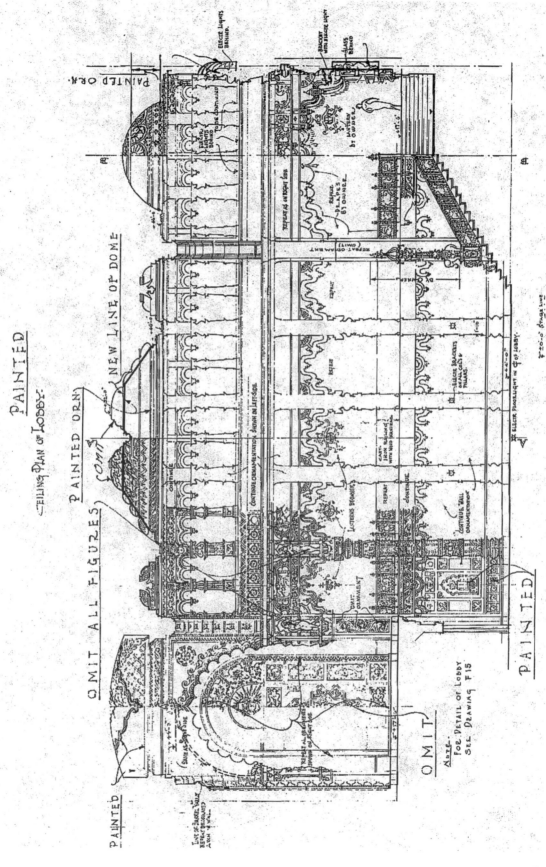

PAINTED

—CEILING PLAN OF LOBBY—

NEW LINE OF DOME

PAINTED ORN.

OMIT ALL FIGURES

PAINTED

PAINTED

OMIT

NOTE—
FOR DETAIL OF LOBBY
SEE DRAWING F 15

9

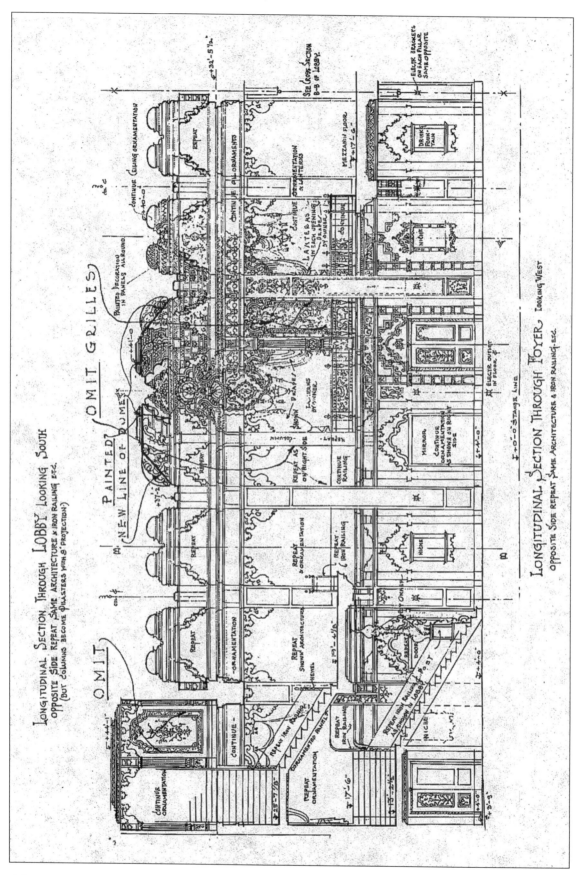

LONGITUDINAL SECTION THROUGH LOBBY LOOKING SOUTH
OPPOSITE SIDE REPEAT SAME ARCHITECTURE & IRON RAILING ETC.
(BUT COLUMNS BECOME PILASTERS WITH 8" PROJECTION)

OMIT GRILLES

PAINTED?
NEW LINE OF DOMES

OMIT

LONGITUDINAL SECTION THROUGH FOYER LOOKING WEST
OPPOSITE SIDE REPEAT SAME ARCHITECTURE & IRON RAILING ETC.

10

Constructing a Masterpiece

After site-clearing, ground was broken on March 25, 1927. Construction, costing some $2 million, took eleven months. Loew, however, never lived to see the result. In frail health, he died of heart failure on Sept. 5, 1927. On the day of his funeral most theaters in the U. S. and Canada closed briefly, then reopened with an orchestral or organ tribute.

Construction-monitoring photos, for Lamb's New York office.   *Landmark Theatre Archive.*

12

Marketing a Masterpiece

Months before completion, space was marketed
and rented in the theater's commercial office wing.

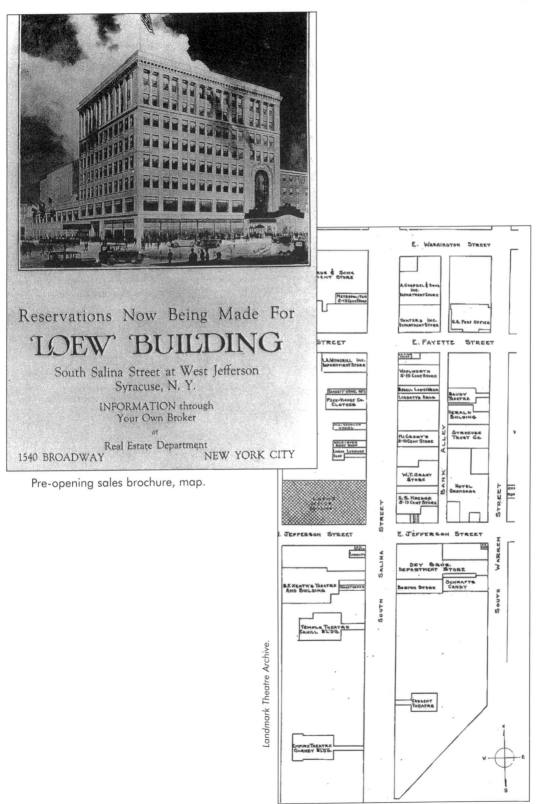

Reservations Now Being Made For

LOEW BUILDING

South Salina Street at West Jefferson
Syracuse, N. Y.

INFORMATION through
Your Own Broker

or

Real Estate Department

1540 BROADWAY   NEW YORK CITY

Pre-opening sales brochure, map.

Landmark Theatre Archive.

Describing a Masterpiece

On completion, Loew's State clearly was a masterpiece— said to be Lamb's favorite work. He replicated it twice in Manhattan, for the Loew's 72d Street theater (since demolished) and Loew's 175th Street (now owned by the church of Rev. Ike). In a lengthy *Motion Picture News* interview accompanied by photos of Loew's State, Lamb explained his design philosophy:

Motion Picture News

In Two Sections
Section Two
June 30, 1928

Revealing Highlights in the History of Motion Picture Theatre Design

An Interview with
THOMAS W. LAMB

A Pioneer and Foremost Theatre
Architect Tells Evolution of
Theatre Planning from Those—

"Good Old Days" to these Better New Days

THOUGH I take the liberty of frankly considering myself among the pioneers in the planning and building of motion picture theatres, I am never tempted—even when cast into a reflective mood such as this interview forces upon me—to regard those early days of my first association with theatre architecture as "The Good Old Days." Indeed, I am one with the theatre patron in believing that these are the Good New Times of theatregoing—what with the improved physical comforts afforded by spacious lobbies, luxurious lounges, restful auditorium chairs, healthful ventilation, unobstructed vision of stage and screen and lighting that is both kind and appealing to the eye.

In the theatre people come to be entertained, but in order that they may be entertained, it is wise to put them in a receptive and friendly frame of mind. This the decorator can do much toward accomplishing. Particularly in the theatre itself, is it his ambition to create a depth and warmth of atmosphere.

To make our audience receptive and interested, we must cut them off from the rest of the city life and take them into a rich and self-contained auditorium, where their minds are freed from their usual occupations and freed from their customary thoughts. In order to do this, it is necessary to present to their eyes a general scheme quite different from their daily environment, quite different in color scheme, and a great deal more elaborate. The theatre can afford this, and must afford it for our public is large, and in the average not wealthy. The theatre is the palace of the average man. As long as he is there, it is his, and it helps him to lift himself out of his daily drudgery.

As another note and departure in theatre decoration the State Theatre, Syracuse, New York, is exceptional in that one feels the full richness and glow of the decorative scheme immediately after having passed through the vestibules.

The styles of architecture vary, but are all permeated with a touch of the Orient, which has always been brightly colorful, emotional and almost seductive in its wealth of color and detail.

The grand foyer is like a temple of gold set with colored jewels, the largest and most precious of which is a sumptuous mural. It represents a festive procession all in Oriental splendor, with elephants, horses, slaves, princes and horsemen, all silhouetted against a deep blue night sky. It is pageantry in its most elaborate form, and immediately casts a spell of the mysterious and to the Occidental mind exceptional.

Using Exotic Ornament

Passing on into the inner foyers and the mezzanine promenade, one continues in the same Indo-Persian style with elaborate ornamentation both in relief and

in painting, all conspiring to create an effect thoroughly foreign to our Western minds. These exotic ornaments, colors and scenes are particularly effective in creating an atmosphere in which the mind is free to frolic and becomes receptive to entertainment.

The auditorium itself is also very much permeated by the Orient, but it is not pure and unadulterated like the foyers and vestibules. It is the European Byzantine Romanesque, which is the Orient as it came to us through the merchants of Venice, those great traders who brought the East and its art back to Europe in their minds, as they brought the cargoes in their ships. The Byzantine and the Romanesque are both European adaptations or distillates of a concoction of the various elements to be found in the East.

"'Good Old Days' to these Better New Days," Thomas W. Lamb, Motion Picture News, June 30, 1928. Theatre Historical Society of America., Elmhurst, Ill.

Landmark gets $2M from state

The grants will allow the theater to expand its stage and restore a box office on Salina Street.

By Mark Bialczak
Staff writer

The Landmark Theatre has received two grants totaling $2 million, the largest one-time allocation in the history of the restored downtown movie palace.

Half the money comes from the newly created State Community Enhancement Program. That money was secured for the theater by Sen. John DeFrancisco, R-Syracuse. DeFrancisco also persuaded Gov. George Pataki to match that amount with a grant from his budget.

"There is nothing more important to the history of culture of this community than the Landmark Theatre," DeFrancisco said Friday during a news conference. "It needed a great infusion of funds."

Secretary of State Sandy Treadwell represented Pataki at the conference in the second-floor lobby of the theater. Treadwell joked that

Pataki wanted to be in Syracu but had a pressing issue — the c ebration honoring the New Yo Yankees World Series victory.

Treadwell read a statement fro Pataki: "The Landmark Theatre a truly historic icon for Syracu and Central New York," he re: "The restoration of this magni cent structure is a reminder of rich history that Syracuse played in the performing arts th continues to this day, and I a pleased that the state can assist t tireless efforts of the Landma Theatre trustees and planni committee.

John Sposato, chairman of Landmark's volunteer board, a past chairman Michael Loguidi traveled to Albany last year champion the theater's cause DeFrancisco. Sposato also n with DeFrancisco and Pataki.

"I'll tell you, when we n with the governor, he basica said that if John DeFrancisco sa this is good for the communi we'll match the funds," Spos said.

DeFrancisco joked that when was growing up in Syracuse,

Ellen M. Blalock / Staff photographer

STATE SEN. John DeFrancisco offers details about how the Landmark Theatre received $2 million from the state at a news conference Friday at the downtown Syracuse theater.

sometimes sneaked in the side door of the theater to watch movies in the balcony.

"I figured this is one way I can pay back the theater," he said.

Sposato said the money will be used to renovate and expand the theater's stage, which will allow bigger Broadway productions to use the theater; install a new theater marquee; renovate the concession and bar area in the downstairs lobby; restore the ticket booth on Salina Street; complete the renovation of all theater doors; restore the upstairs area, including restorations of lighting and fountains; and renovate lobbies and vestibules.

At the end of the conference, state and Landmark officials said they did not wish to comment on the recent debate about the upcoming theater show by shock rocker Marilyn Manson. Mayor Roy Bernardi has said the Nov. 19 performance is inappropriate for the Syracuse community and should not take place. Landmark officials, however, say the show will go on.

"The theater has been in existence for 70 years. Who has been in this theater and who will be in this theater is irrelevant," DeFrancisco said.

Photographing a Masterpiece

Photos on ensuing pages, including views of rare Vanderbilt furnishings removed in the Seventies, suggest the visual riches and esthetic perfection of what Lamb wrought.

Kerry Thurston

Lobby-mezzanine Grand Staircase.

Lobby-mezzanine Grand Staircase.

Lobby mural.

17

Lobby chandelier, Grand Staircase Railing.

Figures on lobby pillars.

Lobby decorative pillars.

Vanderbilt Mansion furnishings before removal; Grand Promenade (mezzanine).

James Foley

James Foley

James Foley

19

Ceramic Backdrop. Grand Promenade Pond.

Dr. Daniel Harris

James Foley

Model Taj Mahal and Vanderbilt table before removal; Grand Promenade.

Grand Promenade Today

James Scherzi

21

Orchestra and Proscenium.

James Scherzi

Auditorium from stage.

Sunburst chandelier over balcony.

Carving said to be Lamb's
face, near auditorium front.

Balcony aisle exit and wall frieze.

South stairway to ground-floor Walnut (now Gifford) Room and Lounges.

James Schug

James Schug

Women's lounge, rest room entrance, Walnut (Gifford) Room.

25

Surviving Vanderbilt Mansion hutch, main lobby.

Railing design around Grand Promenade.

Diverse lighting heightened "fantasy-palace" esthetics.

Lobby "Vanderbilt Chandelier" with Tiffany sconces, before removal.

James Foley

One of central fixtures, Grand Promenade.

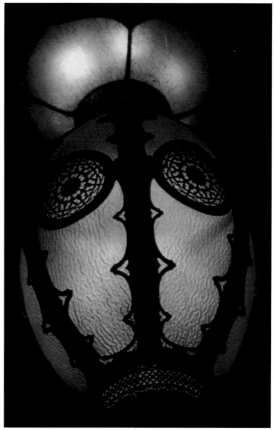

Marie Ryan

Anteroom fixture, Grand Promenade Women's Lounge.

Robert Reep

27

Lobby fixture variation.

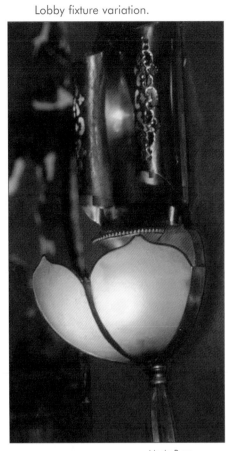

Marie Ryan

Lobby fixture variation.

Marie Ryan

Grand Promenade fixture variation.

Grand Promenade aisle fixture variation.

Burdick and Spitzer

Marie Ryan

Auditorium door, Tiffany glass panel.

James Foley

Auditorium door, Tiffany panel detail.

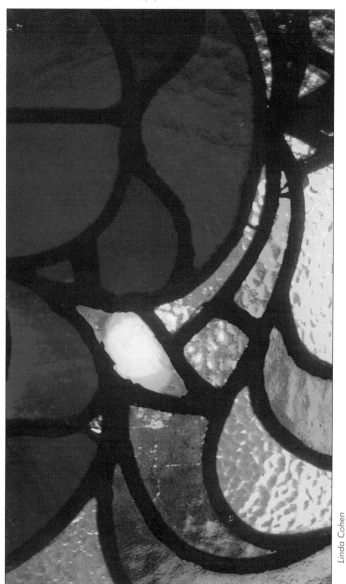

Linda Cohen

Linda Cohen

Tiffany exit sign

29

Fifties marquee replacement for the curvelinear original, beneath the Salina Street facade's crescent window.

James Foley

Original Salina Street three-cashier box office.

James Foley

"Vanderbilt Chandelier" with Tifany sconces before removal, from Musicians Gallery looking toward Garnd Staircase.

Grand Promenade with Vanderbilt Mansion furniture before removal.

32

Walnut (now Gifford) Room with Vanderbilt Mansion furnishings before removal.

33

The 1928, 10-setting Westinghouse light-control board, still in use backstage.

34

Debut of a Masterpiece

The prelude to Loew's State's debut included ads and news-paper stories culminating in the Great Day—Feb. 18, 1928.

Thrill of Homemaking Outdone By Girl in Furnishing Theater

4,500 Yards of Carpet, 5,200 Yards of Draperies and 2,000 Yards of Fringe Purchased by Miss Anne Dornin for New Loew's State.

Post-Standard, Feb. 16, 1928.

The thrill which the ordinary woman gets out of buying a few yards of draperies, two or three large rugs, a few small ones, and enough furniture to fit into the tiny apartment known today as "home," is magnified hundreds of times for Miss Anne H. Dornin, whose task it is to purchase furnishings for all newly constructed Loew theaters. Just now Miss Dornin is concentrating her energies upon Loew's State theater, to open at 11 o'clock Saturday morning.

Forty-five hundred yards of carpet, 5,200 yards of drapery materials, 2,000 yards of fringe and enough gold leaf to cover the entire front of the Loew building, to say nothing of thousands of dollars' worth of rare furniture from China, Japan, India, Cambodia, Java, England, Holland, France, Austria, Belgium and the United States, were personally selected and bought just for this one theater by little Miss Dornin, who started her career as an architect after being graduated from Columbia university, and then went into what she calls "glorified housekeeping."

Place for Each Piece.

At first glance the task of visualizing the furnishing of such a mammoth building seems a colossal one, but Miss Dornin has solved it in a simple way. She goes over the plans carefully, decides just what piece of furniture is to go into each nook and corner, and marks each spot with a number. As each item is purchased it is marked with a number corresponding to its allotted space, and is crossed off the list. If, however, it fails to give the proper effect when the furnishing is completed, it is shifted to a more suitable place.

my theory that the right colorings and furnishings put the theatergoer into a happy mood the minute he or she enters the lobby.

"I like, too, to place here and there some little amusing piece of furniture, to make people laugh. One example of that here will be a tiny lamp, designed as three cuckatoos cuddled up close together, with their eyes blinking." Another is a Chinese god who nods solemnly."

Replica of Taj Mahal.

An interesting importation from India, to be placed in the foyer, is a miniature replica of the Taj Mahal, the beautiful marble mausoleum erected by Shah Jahan in memory of his favorite wife. Still another unusual piece purchased by Miss Dornin is the huge lighting fixture in the new lobby. It was made by Tiffany and for years hung in the Vanderbilt home at Fifty-seventh street and Fifth avenue, New York city.

Miss Dornin has given special care to selection of furnishings for the women's rest and smoking rooms. On [...]

Post-Standard, Feb. 17, 1928.

LOEW'S STATE THEATRE IS READY! ARE YOU?

All roads will lead to LOEW'S STATE THEATRE, SALINA AND JEFFERSON STREETS, tomorrow, when that magnificent playhouse starts to give Syracuse the very best in stage and screen entertainment.

THE DOORS WILL OPEN AT 10 O'CLOCK IN THE MORNING.

AT 11 O'CLOCK—ONE SHORT HOUR AFTER—THE FIRST SHOW WILL COMMENCE. DE LUXE SHOWS SATURDAY AT 1:50, 4:15, 6:35, 9:10.

There will be no reserved seats. The popular "LOEW" prices will prevail. From 11 to 1, admission will be 25c; from 1 to 5, the price will be 35c, and from 5 to closing, the tickets are 50c, with loges at 75c. On Sundays and holidays, the prices vary slightly, with loges selling at 75c.

All daily performances will be continuous from 11 A. M. to 11 P. M. On Sundays the performances will start at 2 P. M. and continue through till 11.

You are going to see, for the FIRST time in Syracuse, the marvelous photoplay, "WEST POINT," with William Haines and Joan Crawford in their best roles.

You are going to see John Murray Anderson's gorgeous production of "MILADY'S FANS," in which many Broadway stars appear. Then there is that bevy of Ada Kaufman Girls. The scenery, the costumes and the stage presentation will dazzle you.

The State Concert Orchestra, conducted by Bruce Brummitt, and the State Serenaders, directed by Ralph Pollack, will play music like you never heard before. Paul Forster, your own favorite organist, will preside at the wonderful Wurlitzer organ. Gee, but you'll be happy when you visit THIS Theatre!

Post-Standard, Feb. 18, 1928.

Secretary Davis Starts Film to Open Loew's at 11 o'Clock

War Chief to Press Button in Washington Office This Morning, Releasing Initial Photoplay Feature at New Syracuse Theater.

Exactly on the stroke of 11 o'clock this morning Dwight W. Davis, secretary of war, in his office in Washington, D. C., will press a button connecting a Postal Telegraph wire with the automatic film projection machines in the Loew's State theater in South Salina street, and "West Point," the initial photoplay attraction at the new playhouse, will begin its premier Syracuse showing. Shortly before 11 the doors will be thrown open for the first time, allowing Syracusans to look upon the magnificence of their new theater.

Formal acceptance of the amusement house will be at 8 o'clock tonight, when Rolland B. Marvin, acting mayor, will give an address of welcome. State and city officials as well as executive officers of the Loew circuit, will be honored guests.

Nicholas M. Schenck, president of Loew's, Inc., who succeeded Marcus Loew, the founder, to that office; Col. E. A. Schiller, v' -presi-

height of 24 feet for especially important scenes. In its ordinary state, the screen is 21 feet wide by 16 feet high. Enlarged, it is one of the largest in the country. To insure smoothness in transition from the small to the larger size, a special arrangement on the projection machines in the booth, picks up a larger lens.

WELL, HERE WE ARE!

LOEW'S STATE THEATRE

OPENS TODAY AT 11 A. M.

And here's the inaugural program.

The FIRST EXCLUSIVE showing of the photoplay "WEST POINT," in which William Haines and Joan Crawford act out the most romantic of love stories.

The stage presentation offers the gorgeous and spectacular John Murray Anderson production, "MILADY'S FAN," in which a cast of Broadway artists, a bevy of beautiful girls and a carload of dazzling scenery will greet your eyes.

The State concert orchestra, with Bruce Brummitt, conducting; the State Syncopators, directed by Ralph Pollock; and the newest type of Wurlitzer organ superbly played by your own favorite, Paul Forster, will be a musical feast.

The description of Loew's State Theatre, as written by the able editorial writer of this newspaper, needs only your own personal inspection for a full realization of its beauty.

Daily, the shows are continuous from 11 to 11.

Sunday, the shows are continuous from 2 to 11.

There will be no reserved seats. The popular "LOEW" prices will prevail. From 11 to 1, admission will be 25c; from 1 to 5, the price will be 35c, and from 5 to closing, the tickets are 50c; with loges at 75c. On Sundays and holidays, the prices will vary slightly, with loges selling at 75c.

Other Theaters Greet NEW LOEW'S STATE

Hearty Greetings and Best Wishes to

LOEW'S

from the

Strand

WALTER D. McDOWELL
Managing Director

TO

LOEW'S

Congratulations
and
Best Wishes

B.F. Keith's

Crescent

A HEARTY WELCOME TO LOEW'S STATE
FROM SALINA STREET'S FIRST HOME OF DE LUXE
PICTURES AND VAUDEVILLE PRESENTATIONS

On The
Stage Tonight
16 Acts
Seven Cash
Prizes

SUNDAY
DOUG MacLEAN
in
"SOFT CUSHIONS"

DAILY THE CITY'S BIGGEST SHOW

Greets

LOEW'S

Syracuse's Newest Theater

Congratulations to

LOEW'S

On Their Fine, New Theater

RIVOLI

MITCHELL FITZER, Manager

SWAN
THE HAPPY HOUR

SYRACUSE THEATRE

Welcomes

LOEW'S

To Syracuse

Landmark Theatre Archive.

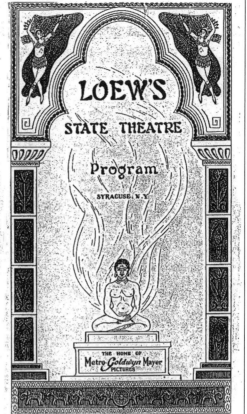

Official Program, distributed Feb. 18, 1928.

FIRE NOTICE—This theatre can be emptied in three minutes. Look around now and choose the nearest exit. In case of fire, Walk (not run) to that Exit.

Souvenir Program

Week Beginning February 18th, 1928

On the Stage

1
OVERTURE
"Slavonic Rhapsody"
The Loew's State Concert Orchestra
BRUCE BRUMMITT
Guest Conductor

2
M-G-M NEWS
News Events of the World and Nation
In Pictures

3
ORGAN CONCERT
"Organs of Yesterday and Today"
PAUL FORSTER

4
Loew's State Theatre presents
"MILADY'S FANS"
Devised and Staged By
JOHN MURRAY ANDERSON

1	**7**
The Lace Fan	*The Italian Fans*
THE ADA KAUFMAN GIRLS	THE ADA KAUFMAN GIRLS
2	**8**
The Feather Fans	HARRY BURNS
BERNICE and EMILY	*Assisted by Tony De Luca*
3	**9**
DOROTHY NEVILLE	*The Jazz Fans*
	BERNICE and EMILY
4	**10**
The Spanish Fan	"Smilin' Thru" Dark Moments
OJEDA and IMBERT	TYLER MASON
5	**11**
"Caprice Basque"	"Humor in Time"
RAE ELEANOR BALL	BENNY and WESTERN
6	**12**
"Serenade"	*Finale*
RAE ELEANOR BALL and	"MILADY'S FAN"
The State Serenaders	

Musical Settings By
RALPH POLLOCK and the STATE SERENADERS

Mason and Hamlin Pianos
Furnished by Clark
Music Co.

On Our Screen

Metro—Goldwyn—Mayer
presents

WILLIAM HAINES

— *in* —

"West Point"

THE CAST

Bruce Wayne......................................	William Haines
Betty Channing..................................	Joan Crawford
Bob Sperry..	Neil Neely
"Tex" McNeill..................................	William Bakewell
Bob Chase..	Ralph Emerson
Captain Munson..................................	Leon Kellar

Directed by EDWARD SEDGWICK
Story by Raymond Schrock

NEXT WEEK   NEXT WEEK

Beginning Saturday
February 25

John GILBERT and Greta GARBO

in

"LOVE"

The Stars of "Flesh and the Devil" Together Again

And Another Sparkling and Colorful Stage Spectacle

"GEMS"

A Mort Harris Production With Glittering Gowns and Gorgeous Girls

---

Landmark Theatre Archive.

37

THRONG IMPRESSED AS THEATER OPENS

THE POST-ST...

SYRACUSE, N. Y. SUNDAY, FEBRUARY

HAYS' AID

THRONG IMPRESSED AS THEATER OPENS

Tense Moments Behind Curtain

Not Only Audience Is Thrilled as Theater Opens.

BY JOSEPH H. ADAMS

OPENING a new theater to the average vaudevillyun is an experience about as soothing as the well-known nervous system as opening a show box with clock-black hand smeared over the wrap-per. But to every rule there is an exception and in the case of the Loew premier yesterday 'Harry Burns, the wop comedjan, was it. Loew opening a new theater than De-Wolf Hopper does of buying a new wedding ring.

"This is my fifth," he said yesterday. I was on the second bill at Keith's six or seven years ago. But, say, there's one opening I'll never forget. That was the new Grand in New York. I think that wax the openingest opening I ever attended. Sit down and I'll give you a load of it."

There was a scream. I nearly fell off the brand new, unpainted chair in the brand new dressing room.

"That's the prim," said Harry.

"The prima?" I said.

"Yes," he said, "the prima donna. She was just gargling a high C."

I settled back in my chair.

"Well, it was just about this kind of a day," said Harry. He glanced out the window at the ...

Dedication Milestone in History of Syracuse, Says Commerce Chamber President.

DECORATIONS OF FOYER ELABORATE

Furnishings and Program Please Large First Day Audiences at Each Performance.

What a theater!
What a memorial to Marcus Loew, and what a bill!

There were those there yesterday and last night at the opening of Loew's State theater who had seen the theater openings of Syracuse for 40 years, but none of them was like this.

Oscar F. Soule, president of the chamber of commerce, said from the stage, "the opening of this theater is a milestone in the history of Syra-cuse."

On an August night in 1889 the Grand was opened. Richard Mans-field in the prime of his greatness as an actor dedicated the Bastable October 2, 1893. The third Wieting, the one of today, was opened Sep-tember 15, 1897. The Empire on March 20, 1911, and Keith's on Jan-uary 27, 1920, followed, each of them finer and better and bigger than any before.

Art of Orient Searched.

Entering Loew's is like walking into some palace that might have been in the days of King Tut or Solomon or Cleopatra. The art of ...

DEATH ACCIDENT, VERDICT IN CASE OF MRS. GORMAN

Body Found Across Range in Clairmonte Avenue Home by Housekeeper.

HEART DISEASE FACTOR

Friends Believe Attorney's Wife Overcome While Preparing Lunch.

One emerging from an open jet in the kitchen range caused the death of Mrs. Marjorie King Gorman, 27, wife of Donald P. Gorman, former assistant corporation counsel, early yesterday at her home, 120 Clairmonte avenue.

Mrs. Marion Kite, housekeeper, found Mrs. Gorman's body, lying partly across the stove, at 7 o'clock yesterday morning when she went to prepare breakfast. One jet was open and the pilot light was out.

The exact circumstances which led to Mrs. Gorman's death probably will never be known, but Coroner Winne stated last night after an investigation that he will give a verdict of "death due to accident."

When Mrs. Gorman was found, ac-cording to William C. Martin, as-sistant district attorney and a close friend of the Gormans, she was in evening dress, indicating that she had gone into the kitchen, presum-ably for a light lunch before retiring, after Mr. Gorman had left her and gone to his room.

In best of spirits, The couple came in at about 11 ...

Screen
Acc...
on

Hays,
La...

THRONG IMPRESSED AS THEATER OPENS

Dedication Milestone in History of Syracuse, Says Commerce Chamber President.

DECORATIONS OF FOYER ELABORATE

Furnishings and Program Please Large First Day Audiences at Each Performance.

What a theater!
What a memorial to Marcus Loew, and what a bill!

There were those there yesterday and last night at the opening of Loew's State theater who had seen the theater openings of Syracuse for 40 years, but none of them was like this.

Oscar F. Soule, president of the chamber of commerce, said from the stage, "the opening of this theater is a milestone in the history of Syra-cuse."

On an August night in 1889 the Grand was opened. Richard Mans-field in the prime of his greatness as an actor dedicated the Bastable October 2, 1893. The third Wieting, the one of today, was opened Sep-tember 15, 1897. The Empire on March 20, 1911, and Keith's on Jan-uary 27, 1920, followed, each of them finer and better and bigger than any before.

Art of Orient Searched.

Entering Loew's is like walking into some palace that might have been in the days of King Tut or Solomon or Cleopatra. The art of China and of India have been searched and copied to give this new-est and finest of Syracuse's theaters its gorgeous fittings and f nishings, its trappings and its dec tions. It is he last word in th cal ap-

Post-Standard, Feb. 19, 1928.

Tense Moments Behind Curtain

Not Only Audience Is Thrilled as Theater Opens.

BY JOSEPH H. ADAMS

OPENING a new theater to the average vaudevillyun is an experience about as soothing to the well-known nervous system as opening a shoe box with clockworks ticking on the inside and a black hand smeared over the wrapper. But to every rule there is an exception and in the case of the Loew premier yesterday Harry Burns, the wop comedian, was it. Harry doesn't think any more of opening a new theater than DeWolf Hopper does of buying a new wedding ring.

"This is my fifth," he said yesterday, "and it's almost my second in Syracuse. I was on the second bill at Keith's six or seven years ago. But, say, there's one opening I'll never forget. That was the new Grand in New York. I think that was the openingest opening I ever attended. Sit down and I'll give you a load of it."

There was a scream. I nearly fell off the brand new, unpainted chair in the brand new dressing room.

"That's the prim," said Harry.

"The prim?" I said.

"Yes," he said, "the prima donna. She was just gargling a high C."

I settled back in my chair.

"Well, it was just about this kind of a day," said Harry. He glanced out the window at the

Post-Standard, Feb. 19, 1928.

Thrills of Theater's Opening Not All Confined to Audience

Activities Back Stage at Zero Hour for Premier Reveal Nervous Tension Among Performers—Something Always Happens.

(Concluded from Page 15)

new, of course, and some of the girls were shy a dressing room."

"Mei Mei Mei Mei Mei"

Over on my left sat a Spanish dancer, morecooing his face until it looked like a mulatto's schoolgirl complexion.

"Just tuning up," explained Harry. I made a mental note to be sure to see him in action, never having heard of a fellow who tangoed on his tonsils.

"WELL, they were shy on dressing rooms," Harry resumed, the while removing his street clothes. "So I gave the girls mine. I fixed up a mirror and table and chair back of the stage. Behind me were two big doors through which they moved the scenery."

Harry was by now attired in his Paris garters with a reminiscent look in his face to match.

"Well, it seems that the theater has a nifty ventilation system," he went on, removing the socks and easing away from the window. "You just simply pushed a button and every window and door in the theater opened. It was a good system. The only fault I had to find with it was that the button was pushed just at the moment when I was as I am now."

He shivered a little as he got into his comic underwear and threw his wop suit on the floor for something to stand on.

"And I want to tell you that when those two doors back of me opened I didn't have to turn around to find it out. All the winter in that neighborhood, and there was plenty, just rushed right in and swarmed all over my personality. I never felt so out of character in all my life!"

He stepped off his comic suit and got into it. The old suit has to double for a bath mat. Harry says that when he dresses standing on the checkers he can move around better. Furthermore, he added, if you don't step on those loud suits once in a while they won't pipe down during the act.

how painfully prophetic his words were.

Down the stairs we went, Tony gingerly carrying the basket of balloons and Harry walking stiff and erect so the trick hat he was wearing would keep its balance. And in the wings we watched the various acts and listened to the laughter which floated backstage like the wind through a forest or the handclapping which sounded like a patter of hail on a tin roof.

Breathlessly, the dancing girls waited to go on and even more breathlessly they came off. Through it all ran a distinct undercurrent of nervous tension, a terrific strain generated by the artists' anxiety as to whether their offerings would please the hundreds who sat as tho on a red plush throne in the gilded palace out front and dared those behind the scenes to come out and make them surrender their dignity.

And there was plenty of dignity out there, too; people can't be ushered through a glittering temple by uniformed ushers with ramrods for backbones and a royal kowtow for every direction they gave without finding it a little difficult to be so vulgar as to laugh right out loud in front of everybody.

But they did, and it was worth the expenditure for toy balloons to Burns to draw the laughs which each explosion, accompanied by Harry's wop dialect, drew. As the act drew to a close and Harry began telephoning to the morgue for a friend who was drowned a couple of weeks ago but maybe he no come up yet, his partner, Tony, came limping off the stage. He had stepped on a nail and the more he scraped to get it out of his shoe the deeper it sunk. Yes, something always goes wrong on opening night.

On the way out I asked the stage door attendant where Paul Forster was parked. I might just as well have asked the number of Charlie Chaplin's election district

"He doesn't know," said Burns. "He's a stranger here himself."

SOMETHING TO BOAST ABOUT.

Feb. 18, 1928

An English dramatist once wrote an "Apology for Actors." But that was several hundred years ago. Nowadays neither the theater nor its people need apology. The stage folk can lay claim to large professional progress; and the theater has advanced and developed to a degree which would have been unthinkable, even a few years ago. The stage is increasingly an institution in our life.

But Syracuse finds no warrant for apology. Just now it is prepared to boast. Loew's State Theater, to which the public will have its first regular admission today, stands a conspicuous addition to the group of imposing structures which mark the heart of the newer, busier Syracuse. It is monument to enterprise in which there is investment of millions. It provides notably attractive accommodations for 3,000 people. It is designed to couple luxury with entertainment. And the record of the Loew theaters in other cities is evidence of the high grade which can be expected to mark that entertainment.

Here we have the most modern in theater arrangement. Facilities exceed all that have prevailed in the past. Safety is provided for in full measure. In scarlet and gold, the interior makes arresting appeal to the eye. Objects of art are brought in to give an effect new to the theater. All is intelligently contrived to suggest an oriental atmosphere. Operating equipment is the best which stagecraft up to the present time has been able to devise.

Altogether Loew's State Theater is elaborately and carefully prepared for the attainment of its objective: A good show in a good environment.

It will open with representatives of the operating company in New York here for personal observation of the inauguration of the notable enterprise. It will unquestionably open with welcoming Syracusans crowding its doors, eager to become acquainted with a playhouse which is bound to figure largely in the years we have ahead of us.

The State has the good wishes of all Syracuse.

Editorial, Feb. 18, 1928.

Post-Standard, Feb. 20, 1928.

LOEW'S STATE THEATRE OPENS
SALINA AT JEFFERSON ST.

They gathered in groups inside the theatre.

They stood in crowds outside the theatre.

Some talked to others in audible whispers. Others spoke to some right out loud in meetin'.

But they all seemed to be saying the one thing.

Each was trying to think up words to describe the beauty, the splendor, the richness of LOEW'S STATE THEATRE. Each was trying to find a word that would be a fitting description of the great photoplay, "WEST POINT," which they had just seen for the FIRST time; they also tried to explain the gorgeousness of the stage show, "MILADY'S FAN," which John Murray Anderson conceived and produced.

Praise was heaped upon the grand concert orchestra, directed so superbly by Bruce Brummitt; there were words of commendation for the marvelous stage band so ably conducted by Ralph Pollack; the organ selections by Paul Forster received much approbation. Indeed, the entire show, from beginning to end, had more than fulfilled all the wonderful things said about it.

But though all were praising the show and the beautiful theatre, each was also agreeably surprised to know that such abundant and entertaining performances can be seen at these popular "LOEW" prices. Daily, from 11 to 1, the price is 25 cents; from 1 until 5, the admission is but 35 cents, and from 5 until closing, the tickets are 50 cents. In the evening, special loge seats are available at 75 cents.

Sundays and holidays, the prices vary slightly.

There are no reserved seats. The performances are continuous from 11 a. m. to 11 p. m.

LOEW'S STATE THEATRE, its stage and screen entertainment, its service and its entrancing atmosphere, compel you to make a visit there THIS WEEK.

The name LOEW'S is pronounced as "LOW'S."

LOEW'S STATE THEATRE IS GRATEFUL—

Grateful to the thousands of citizens of Syracuse and its environs who filled this huge and beautiful new theatre at all the opening performances on last Saturday, and every day since—and who, we hope, were perfectly entertained by the inaugural stage and screen program presented.

Grateful, too, are we to the City of Syracuse as represented by such dignitaries as Mayor Charles G. Hanna; Acting Mayor Rolland B. Marvin, who delivered the dedicatory address; President of the Chamber of Commerce, Oscar T. Soule; the Chiefs of the Police and Fire Departments, their deputies, captains, lieutenants and members together with all the other city and civic officials and the various newspapers who lent such co-operative and cordial aid in making the inaugurating of the new Loew's State Theatre such an auspicious and happy occasion.

To our neighboring theatres and their managers and owners—B. F. Keiths, the Empire, the Strand, the Eckel, the Wieting, the Temple and the many others—we wish to bow grateful acknowledgment for the many kind wishes.

In conclusion we say again, to the citizens of Syracuse, LOEW'S STATE THEATRE is yours. May it bring you endless days of pleasure and happiness.

LOEW'S INC.

Post-Standard, Feb. 21, 1928.

Silents, 'Talkies,' Stage Shows

Loew's State was built to present silent movie/vaudeville bills, accompanied by its "Mighty Wurlitzer," with its four manuals (full keyboard tiers) and twenty ranks (sets) of pipes. But the month after the theater's debut, its Lillian Gish silent, "The Enemy," was upstaged by Eckel and Strand bills featuring synchronized-phonograph sound. Loew's first sound presentations, Movietone shorts with a soundtrack invented in Auburn, arrived in August. Its first full-length soundtrack feature, MGM's Oscar-winning "The Broadway Melody," opened in March, 1929.

Post-Standard, Aug. 11, 1928.

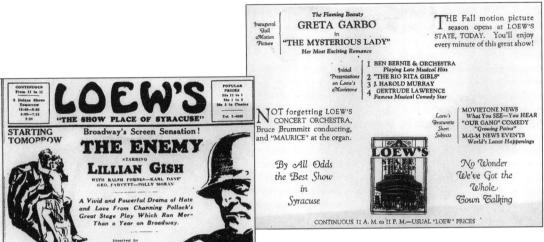

Post-Standard, March 16, 1928.

Post-Standard, March 30, 1929.

Stars, Stars, Stars

Before the Depression and "talkies" combined to kill national vaudeville circuits, a succession of stars graced Loew's stage. These included Beatrice Lillie, Sophie Tucker, Jack Benny, and Milton Berle. Berle's autobiography told of being summoned from Loew's State for his "big break"—to emcee at vaudeville's renowned Palace Theatre in Manhattan. Film siren Jean Harlow appeared at Loew's in 1932. Syracuse's first public demonstration of TV occurred on Loew's stage in 1933.

Post-Standard, Sept. 8, 1928.

Post-Standard, March 29, 1930.

Post-Standard, May 8, 1931.

The Golden Years

In the Twenties through the Forties, going downtown by trolley, bus, auto, or on foot was an Event, and seeing a movie an Occasion. At Loew's a uniformed "barker"— doorman— presided at curbside. Three boxoffice cashiers sold tickets. Uniformed ushers hovered over velvet-roped waiting lanes. New features arrived weekly. Films played from midday to midnight. Normal fare included a newsreel, cartoon, travelogue, or other "short." "Gone With the Wind" and other megahits sold out.

Loew's was a self-contained community, with management offices, an organist, stage crews, a carpenter's shop, ushers' dressing room, and parts, scenery, and other basement storage cubicles. The theater was a focus for parades, stars' visits, and other movie premiere events. During World War II it staged recruitment and Savings Bond promotions. "Loew's," as one resident put it, "was central to our lives."

Salina Street with "Theater Row."

Loew's student ushers corps.

Post-Standard, Aug. 18, 1939.

Onondaga Historical Association.

TOMORROW MORNING 10 A.M.

Syracuse gets its first view of

GONE WITH THE WIND

COME ANYTIME TOMORROW FROM 10 A.M. UP TO 2:45 P.M. AND SEE A COMPLETE PERFORMANCE

NO SEATS RESERVED for tomorrow's matinee or for any weekday matinees ... continuous performances

GALA RESERVED SEAT PREMIERE TOMORROW 8 P.M.

Gone With The Wind will be shown here in its entirety, exactly as presented at Atlanta and Broadway premieres. While this engagement is limited this production will not be shown anywhere except at advanced prices—at least until 1941

BUY RESERVED SEATS NOW

FOR THE GALA PREMIERE TOMORROW NIGHT AND ALL OTHER NIGHT SHOWS

NIGHT SHOWS (8 P.M.) ALL SEATS RESERVED **$1.10 incl. tax**
(EXCEPT LOGES)

SUNDAY MAT. (2 P.M.) ALL SEATS RESERVED **$1.10 incl. tax**
(EXCEPT LOGES)

WEEKDAY MATS. CONTINUOUS NOT RESERVED **75c incl. tax**
(EXCEPT LOGES)

DAVID O. SELZNICK'S *production of* MARGARET MITCHELL'S
Story of the Old South

GONE WITH THE WIND

In TECHNICOLOR *starring*
CLARK GABLE
as Rhett Butler

LESLIE HOWARD · OLIVIA De HAVILLAND
and presenting
VIVIEN LEIGH
as Scarlett O'Hara

A SELZNICK INTERNATIONAL PICTURE · *Directed by* VICTOR FLEMING
Screen Play by SIDNEY HOWARD · Music by Max Steiner
A Metro-Goldwyn-Mayer Release

LOEW'S THEATRE

Post-Standard, Feb. 24, 1940.

The Music Changes

Movie-chain revenues peaked about 1947. Then TV, suburbia, and shopping malls, combined with a ban on joint studio-theater ownerships, ended the movie palace era. Multi-screen, bare-wall theater complexes eclipsed larger moviehouses. In 1959 the Strand—a Loew's "rollover" (second-run) house since the Forties—was demolished for a parking garage. The Empire went next. In 1965, months after being restored for a last concert, the long-unused Loew's Wurlitzer was sold. The Paramount closed in 1966, and Keith's in 1967. The Eckel became The Biograph, and it and Loew's went "downmarket," with Loew's even experimenting with adults-only films. Downtown movies seemed passe.

Herald-Journal, Aug. 23, 1959.

Wreckers Take Over The Strand

Another chapter in Syracuse theater history came to a close last Sunday when Loew's Strand closed its doors for the final time with the last showing of "A Hole in the Head," starring Frank Sinatra.

The Strand, being torn down to provide additional city parking facilities, began operations March 17, 1914 under the management of Edgar Weill. Those were the days when the city's theater row carried such names as Bastable, the Crescent, the Temple, the Hippodrome, the Wieting, the Empire and the Eckel.

... a motion picture ... also one

Face Demolition
Keith's, Paramount Hope to Relocate

Post-Standard, July 14, 1966.

RKO Keith's and Paramount theaters, scheduled to be demolished in urban renewal plans, are still "up in the air" as to when this will occur. However, both theaters want relocate in downtown Syracuse if suitable sites can be ...nd.

...oth Harry Unterfort, zone ...ager of Schine theaters, Dave Levin, manager of Keith's, said yesterday is yet no definite offers been made for their ...ies for UR purposes, as to operating time two theaters' varies ...ober to Jan. 1. ...ant to stay in Syra...d Mr. Levin. "Syra... growing area and ...rish to leave here." ...ort declared that ...e. ...yracuse should be ...n ever with new ...re Edwards depart...ner Dey's and the ...fore re.
...ew's unt and Keith's ...le than 40 years have backstage facil...ce they were moti... closing and vaudev...

the only remaining downtown motion picture theater with facilities for live stage presentations will be Loew's.

Post-Standard, Aug. 9, 1960.

It's Curtains For Historic Theater Today

The Empire theater, at long last, will succumb to becoming a parking garage, closing its doors today. Opened in 1911, the Empire was the scene of many an important Bro... try-out, before it ... movie house.
For ...

Herald-American, Feb. 23, 1964.

Public Gets Bid to Concert On Old Theater Pipe Organ

The sweeping swells and sustained crescendos of the old theater pipe organ that was as necessary to the melodrama of the silent flicks as the handlebar mustache on the villainous landlord, will sound again in Syracuse.

Next Sunday morning the only remaining theater pipe organ in operating condition in the area will let out its stops after a 10-year silence. The public is invited to Loew's State Theater to reminisce.

The organ installed in 1926 in Loew's was uncovered a few months ago by members of the American Association of Theater Organ Enthusiasts. It was just five months ago that they began their afterhours restoration.

About 10 members met weekend mornings at the Salina street theater and then returned after the ... vie let out for the ... sometimes worked ...T. Anderson, one ...bbyists said.
...the fo...

The manager of Loew's, Sam Gilman, is opening the theater to the public for the free program. He recalls that the last time the organ was heard there was during intermissions of the Saturday evening shows 10 years ago.

tuned the glockenspiel, xylophone, marimba and even the bird whistles, horses hoofs and surf sounds which distinguish the weighty theater organ.

Next Sunday at 9:30 a.m. the four-manual, horseshoe-shaped console in its gleaming white paint will rise on a lift from the orchestra pit in condition as near original as the enthusiasts could effect.

Dean Robinson, who played for silent movies during the late 1920s will pump out the old favorites as the over 1,400 pipes varying in height from two inches to 16 feet located behind grillwork on both sides of the auditorium, project the thrilling timbres.

"It's amazing how many people don't realize the power of a theater organ," Anderson said. "It's nothing like an electronic or home-styled organ."

But the organist won't be testing the volume next Sunday. "It would drive everyone out of the theater if he did," said Anderson.

...familiar to the late Jesse Craw...ford.

End of elegant showplace
Final curtain will fall at Keith's theater

Herald-American, Jan. 1, 1967.

Full of years and honors, Keith's is scheduled to succumb to the wrecker's maul in April. It will dim its lights forever Thursday night.

Down will come the structure, built at a cost of more than two million dollars, with

...ville stars, Milton Berle, recalled to a Herald-American reporter last summer that he played the Syracuse Keith's in the early 1920's and audiences here were among the toughest in the country.

He remembered that the hotel in which he was staying caught fire and "I went back

47

At the Brink

Amid demolition of movie palaces nationwide, Loew's State's appeared doomed. A 1967 headline warned of its possible razing—forestalled by a subsequent tax cut. But its downward slide continued, culminating in announcement of its closing in May, 1975.

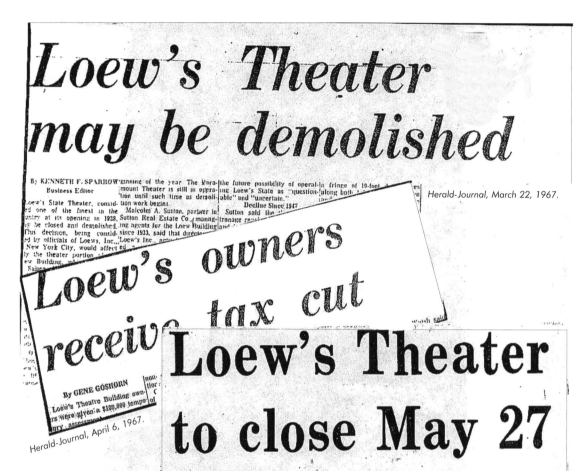

Loew's Theater may be demolished

By KENNETH F. SPARROW
Business Editor

...ginning of the year. The Para-mount Theater is still in opera-tion until such time as demoli-tion work begins.

Loew's State Theater, consid-...d one of the finest in the ...untry at its opening in 1928, ...y be closed and demolished. This decision, being consid-...d by officials of Loews, Inc., New York City, would affect ...ly the theater portion ...w Building.

...the future possibility of opera-ble" and "uncertain."

Malcolm A. Sutton, partner in Sutton Real Estate Co., manag-ing agents for the Loew Building since 1933, said that director...

Decline Since 1947

Sutton said the ...frontage ...

...tion fringe of 19-foot ...question along both ...

Herald-Journal, March 22, 1967.

Loew's owners receive tax cut

By GENE GOSHORN

Loew's Theatre Building own-ers were given a $100,000 tempo-rary assessment...

Herald-Journal, April 6, 1967.

Loew's Theater to close May 27

By A. BROHMANN ROTH

Loew's State Theater, the last of the grand palaces of entertainment in downtown Syracuse, will close its door Tuesday, May 27.

Announcement of the the-ater's demise was made to-day by Malcolm A. Sutton, partner in Sutton Real Es-tate Co., and managing agents for the Loew Build-ing since 1933.

He said he received word from Arthur Raporte, vice president in charge of real estate, at the New York City Loew headquarters.

Employes of the theater were notified of the closing date today.

The closing order affects the theater only, Sutton said. As to what will be done with it is not known, Sutton explaining that at present there are no defi-nite plans for the future as to whether it will be con-verted into office space.

The theater, reputed to be one of the finest in the coun-try, opened with vaudeville acts and a motion picture in 1928, its 3,100 seats filled by a black tie crowd.

Back in 1967 Loew's was considering closing the the-ater but kept it going at the insistance of city officials

and civic leaders. But it has been on a downhill slide of since.

Sutton said the theater's patronage reached its peak in 1947 and since then, espe-cially the last few years, continued operation of the theater became economic-ally unfeasible.

The building has a fron-tage on South Salina Street of 125 feet and the same on the Clinton Street side. The office portion extends 100 feet on the Jefferson street side. The remaining 170 feet

along Jefferson is occupied by the theater.

Of the 125 feet frontage on Salina Street, 35 feet is occupied by the theater. The balance is held by stores.

The theater takes in the first through fourth floors of the building.

The closing of the theater will have no effect on the presentation of the Pom-peian Players "Fiddler on the Roof" May 15-19 and other commitments the the-ater may have.

Herald-Journal, May 7, 1975.

City Council member Armand Magnarelli, since retired, recalls the next developments:

"I was on the Syracuse Common Council when I received a call from a source at City Hall. He said, 'Hey, Armand, did you know that they're inquiring about a demolition permit for the inside of Loew's Theatre?'

"I have always had an interest in Loew's—I was an usher there for four years and knew the theater inside-out. I called Malcolm Sutton, [who was its property manager]. He said, 'Well, what we've got in mind, we're going to demolish the theater, because it's not doing enough business, and we're going to make a parking garage inside the building.'

"I talked to Lee Alexander, who was the Mayor, had no interest in the arts and traveled a lot, leaving many decisions to me. He said, 'Do what you want to do.' So I made some phone calls. I got about twelve people that I knew would be interested in saving that building. Jay King [Joseph H. King Jr. of Bache & Co.] agreed to co-chair. I told the group what happened and said,'We can't allow them to do this. If we lose the Loew's we lose the heart of downtown.'"

Committee formed to save Loew's

Efforts will be made to convince Loew's Inc. to extend its deadline for closing the 47-year-old Loew's State Theater in downtown Syracuse.

The owners have announced their intention to close the landmark show place next Tuesday because it is an unprofitable operation.

Joseph H. King Jr., president of Landmarks Association of Central New York, said his Citizens Committee to Save Loew's will contact the owners this week in an effort to get an extension of the May 27 closing date.

The theater, which opened as a film and vaudeville house in 1928, has been losing money for the corporation in recent years.

A similiar threat to close the theater and demolish it in 1967 was stalled by a reak and civic support.

King, cochairman of the committee with Common Councillor Armand Magnarelli, said the pledge to meet with

Loew's executives on the closing was one of the suggestions produced in the new group's first meeting yesterday.

The committee, which numbered about 20 members as of Tuesday, decided to ask Sutton Real Estate Co., managers of the Loew Building, to contact the owners to discuss extending the closing and request that nothing be removed from the theater "until a solution can be worked out."

As a result of enthusiasm shown at the meeting, King said he is personally confident "there is a good chance of finding a solution to the problem." As far as he is concerned, that solution involves continued operation of Loew's as a movie house with theater and concert bookings.

The 3,100-seat theatre is considered a gem of its type, not only in terms of its lush 30s decor, but for its stage facilities.

"I think the committee has the enthusiasm, imagination and expertise to solve the problem," King said. "It's going to happen."

In addition to the effort with the owners, a subcommittee headed by Murray Bernthal of Famous . Artists will look into the entertainment aspects of the matter while another chaired by John Searles . of Metropolitan Development Association will investigate taxes and a ٪ sessments.

The committee, which was formed after an "unprecedented number of requests to help save Loew's" was received by the Landmarks Association, will meet again June 3.

Meanwhile, King said, the . Greater Syracuse Chamber of Commerce has agreed to act as a clearinghouse for the effort. He urged residents interested in helping to contact the chamber offices.

Herald-Journal, May 21, 1975.

The clandestine sale of the theater lobby's elegant "Vanderbilt Chandelier" energized citizen efforts.

Councilman Magnarelli recalls:

"Our group had at least six or seven meetings, and finally decided maybe we should buy the entire building. The rents we receive would help offset the theater's costs. I met with Sutton, who was one of my good friends. I told him, 'I've got to get a price. I've got to get the income statements, is it brought up to code, all the details.' A week went by, two weeks, I said, 'Malcolm, we're going to have another meeting, I've got to have that information.'

"One thing we didn't know: The main chandelier was Tiffany. One day I'm in the theater, and see them taking this chandelier down. I thought they were going to move it from one place to another. Later I was told somebody in California had bought it and paid Loew's $10,000. Actually it was a fellow in Syracuse with a woman as partner. I couldn't believe it."

Chandelier Disappears From Loew's

By NEVART APIKIAN

The Vanderbilt Chandelier has been removed from Loew's Theater, closed since Tuesday.

After tracing the story for two days, it was confirmed from New York city headquarters of Loew's that two Syracusans purchased the elaborate lighting fixture.

However, the head of Loew's real estate was initially unaware of its removal, as was the local real estate agent.

Malcolm Sutton, in charge of Loew's real estate here, said: "I was promised that nothing would be removed until people here could have a chance to work and see what they could come up with in the way of saving Loew's."

The theater, built in 1928, and one of the last of the area's opulent movie palaces, finally closed Tuesday after several years of probable closing notices.

Meanwhile, civic leaders as well as cultural leaders are

Post-Standard, June 4, 1975.

Chandelier Sparks 'Save Loew's' Efforts

Committee Explores Rescue Strategies

By DOROTHY NEWER

Community efforts to restore the sparkling crystal chandelier to the darkened lobby of Loew's Theater on Salina Street were launched yesterday at a meeting of a Greater Syracuse Chamber of Commerce "Save Loew's" committee.

The chandelier was dismantled and removed from the lobby after having been sold to local glass dealers David Jenks and Linda O'Leary for a reported $10,000.

The sale was made by a Loew executive who apparently was unaware another top official of the company had assured Malcolm Sutton, local manager of Loew's real estate interests here, that "nothing would be disturbed" following the theater's official closing May 27.

The chandelier is said to have been made by Louis Tiffany for the Fifth Avenue home of Cornelius Vanderbilt. It is not clear how it wound up hanging in Loew's lobby when the theater was opened in 1928. In recent years, because of energy-saving efforts it has not been lighted.

Mrs. O'Leary, one of the purchasers, says some alterations had been made in the fixture and some of the prisms had been broken off it since it adorned the Vanderbilt home. She declined to say what the plans for the chandelier are, pending return to Syracuse from Chicago of her business associate, Jenks.

According to one source, the chandelier is still in Syracuse awaiting shipment to the Parke-Bernet Galleries in New York City. Estimates of the chandelier's value range from $40,000 to "priceless."

"The chandelier is just one item. Loew's is still a great the

Post-Standard, May 31, 1975.

50

Attendee list for the charter "Citizens Committee to Save Loew's" meeting on May 20, 1975:

LANDMARKS ASSOCIATION OF CENTRAL NY

CITIZENS COMMITTEE TO SAVE LOEW'S

ORGANIZATION MEETING

AGENDA

I. Introduction of Committee Members and Others Present

II. Explanation of the Problem
   Mr. Malcolm Sutton

III. Development of Potential Solutions
   "Brainstorming" : List of Ideas
   Appointment of Sub-Committees

IV. Schedule Report Meeting

V. Adjourn

CITIZENS COMMITTEE TO SAVE LOEW'S

Armand Magnarelli, Chairman
First Trust & Deposit Co.
201 So. Warren St.
Syracuse NY 13202
Ofc. 424-2383

Joseph H. King, Jr., Co-Chairman
Bache & Co., Inc.
One Mony Plaza
Syracuse NY 13202
Ofc. 424-1443

Mrs. Susan Snook
Greater Syracuse Chamber of Commerce
One Mony Plaza
Syracuse NY 13202
Ofc. 422-1343

Mr. Albert R. Babinicz
Central N. Y. Regional Transportation
Authority
508 Midtown Plaza
700 East Water St.
Syracuse NY 13202
Ofc. 471-2100

Mr. Nicholas J. Pirro
N. Y. State Division of Housing &
Community Renewal
State Office Bldg.
Syracuse NY 13202
Ofc. 473-8115

Mr. James J. Wilson
Wilsons Jewelers
So. Salina St.
Syracuse NY 13202
Ofc. 422-9141

Dr. Joseph Golden
Cultural Resources Council
113 E. Onondaga St.
Syracuse NY 13202
Ofc. 471-1761

Mr. Thomas O. Mehen
Sibleys
400 South Salina St
Syracuse NY 13202
Ofc. 637-5911

Mr. Sam J. Mitchell
Carriage House East
Manlius NY 13104
H. 682-2191

Mr. N. Richard Hueber
473 Westcott St.
Syracuse NY 13210
Ofc. 474-5241

Mr. Peter Baum
403 Seitz Bldg.
Syracuse NY 13202
Ofc. 422-8288

Mr. William Knowlton
U.S. Army District Recruiting
700 East Water St
Syracuse NY 13210
Ofc. 473-3407

Mr. John Coffey
S.O.C.P.A.
300 East Fayette St.
Syracuse NY 13202
Ofc. 477-7333

Mr. John R. Searles Jr.
Metropolitan Development Assoc.
State Tower Bldg.
Syracuse NY 13202
Ofc. 422-8284

Mr. John D. Quinlivan
Q.P.K. Architects
101 East Water St.
Syracuse NY 13202
Ofc. 472-7806

Ms. Joey Nigro
Volunteer Center
103 East Water St.
Syracuse NY 13202
Ofc. 474-7011

Staying the Course

An endurance test began. Over the next fifteen months, Loew's won new tax concessions; it reopened the theater; rescuers incorporated as the Syracuse Area Landmark Theatre (SALT); and Loew's announced the theater's "final" closing, in September, 1976.

Armand Magnarelli recalls:

"One day I got a call from New York. The caller said, 'Armand, did you know Loew's Theatre has been sold?' I called Sutton and said, 'I heard a rumor that it's been sold.' 'Yeah,' he said, 'I bought it. I thought it would be best for everybody.'

"I said, 'What'd you buy it for?' He said, '125 thousand.' I said, 'Jeez, we were talking 300, 325 thousand for the building....Our group would have bought it for 125 thou-sand.' He said, 'Well, you can buy the theater portion of it.' I said, 'What do you want for it?' He said, '110 thousand dollars.' [We exchanged some harsh words;] he threw me out.'

"The committee appointed a group to deal with Sutton....Its secretary Peter Baum was our lawyer. If anybody deserves special credit for what was done, he's the guy. He was the key."

Herald-Journal, July 7, 1975.

Loew's to reopen minus chandelier

Post-Standard, July 10, 1975.

Loew's Group Okays Firm

'Save Loew's' Group Gains Regents' Nod

Post-Standard, July 7, 1976.

Post-Standard, Aug. 10, 1976.

SALT Starts Survey in 'Save Loew's' Proposal

Herald-Journal, Sept. 8, 1976.

Loew's up for sale

Herald-Journal, Oct. 15, 1976.

Suttons buy Loew Building

Loew's era ends tonight

Herald-Journal, Sept. 28, 1975.

By RICHARD G. CASE

The lights go out at Syracuse's Loew's Theatre tonight — again.

Whether they are re-lit remains a question.

Loew's Corp. of New York...both theatre and...has b...

City Corporation Counsel Edward Kearse said today the deal is off, because the corporation did not keep its bargain and maint... on operation of the theatre by the nonpro-

52

Sutton's asking price for the theater—$100,000—seemed beyond
SALT's reach. But it persevered, nearing success in Summer, 1977.

Herald-Journal, March 2, 1977.

Drive to save Loew's Theater broadens

National landmark status may not save Loew's

Herald-Journal, May 12, 1977.

Loew's Theater has been declared a national landmark.

The Salina Street "movie palace" was added to the National Register of Historic Places by action of the U.S. Interior Department May 3.

Notification of the listing was made to the Landmarks Association of Central New York today.

The theater, which opened in 1928, has been the focus of a campaign to save it. The property, part of the downtown Loew Building, faces demolition and it is not known what impact landmark registry will have on future plans.

Application for landmark status was made in March 1975 by Richard Buchanan of the Syracuse University Architecture Research Department.

Formal nomination came from the State Landmarks Board.

Approval of the nomination by the federal board means both possible financial benefits and drawbacks, depending on future developments. Federal funds could be made available for preservation but demolition could mean financial penalties to the owner.

The listing does not automatically guarantee preservation, according to experts.

The theater, which showed first-run films for many years, was closed by Loew's Corp. in September 1976. Revenue losses were cited.

Last November, the entire building, including the closed theater, was purchased by Sutton Real Estate of Syracuse, which had been managing agent since the structure was completed.

Malcolm Sutton, chairman of the firm, said last week he and his partners felt negotiations to save the theater portion had broken down and they were pursuing other options, including demolition of the old movie house.

Sutton had offered to sell the theater to the Syracuse Area Landmarks Theater organization, a private citizens group, for $100,000.

The group, known as SALT, last week decided the price was too high, but chairman Eleanor Shopiro said she didn't feel hopes to preserve Loew's had died with withdrawal of the offer.

Sutton said the firm does not have the expertise to operate the theater and wanted to sell the structure. If this is not possible, he said the 3,800-seat auditorium wing would be demolished.

If the theater was razed, the realtor said the lobby might be developed as store space, with a Salina Street entrance. The empty theater portion would be used as a parking lot but held for future development.

Sutton said he felt the firm had given SALT enough time to find an alternative to demolition.

Experts familiar with National Register listing said the owner of a landmark structure cannot claim demolition as a business deduction on taxes ... razed landmark; thereby discouraging commercial development of the site.

On the other hand, according to a memo from the Syracuse-Onondaga Planning Agency, the listing would make the owner of Loew's Theater eligible for matching grant-in-aid federal funds on a 50-50 U.S.-local share basis for acquisition, rehabilitation and architectural and technical services.

SALT, a month ago, mounted a membership campaign to support its preservation drive. Mrs. Shopiro said over $3,000 has been raised to date with about 500 single and family ...

She said she planned to meet with city officials and downtown business leaders in an effort to assay that interest.

"If we don't get that support from influencial groups, the project may have to be abandoned," she added.

Loew's is considered one of the few remaining "movie palaces" left in the U.S. Architect Thomas Lamb, who specialized in the type, considered it his "finest achievement."

Buchanan, in his application, said Loew's was built in ...

$5,000 for Loew's
Grant to fund restoration study

By RICHARD G. CASE

A grant of $5,000 to study the architectural possibilities of restoring Loew's Theater in downtown Syracuse has been awarded by the National Endowment for the Arts.

The grant comes at a time when future of the Salina Street landmark is in doubt.

Malcolm Sutton, chairman of the firm that owns the theater and surrounding office building, said today he expects estimates of demolition costs later this week.

Meanwhile, Mrs. Eleanor Shopiro, chairman of Syracuse Area Landmark Theater (SALT), announced receipt of the $5,000 NEA grant.

"Worthwhile Cause"

"We got exactly what we applied for," Mrs. Shopiro explained. "I feel that's a reflection of the fact NEA thought this was an immensely worthwhile cause."

She said SALT asked for the grant to finance architectural studies of the theater, which is considered one of the last of the opulent "movie palaces" that opened in 1928 and was closed and sold by Loew's Corp. to Sutton Real Estate last ... with it was declared a national ... federal government ... be held

Herald-Journal, July 7, 1977.

A membership drive to enlist citizen support for SALT has raised about $3,000 to date with about 500 single and family members enrolled.

Willing to Sell

Sutton said last month his firm is willing to sell the theater and separate it from the rest of the Loew Building. Asking price: $100,000.

The realtor explained that his staff doesn't have the expertise to run a theater and feels SALT has been given a reasonable length of time to come up with an alternative to demolition.

Plans developed by the realtor would raze the theater portion while keeping the lobby. The empty space would be used for parking and the lobby portion, with the Salina Street "marquee" entrance, renovated for stores.

In addition to demolition estimates, Sutton also has obtained an antique dealer's appraisal of the value of fixtures remaining in the theater if they are sold.

Dismay Expressed

When the national landmark listing, which had been applied for in 1975, was announced, Sutton expressed dismay, saying the designation had not been sought and might interfer with redevelopment plans for the site.

... listing clears the way for federal ... ation grants while, at the same ... ouraging commercial develop... ... allowing certain tax breaks ... ...dmark structures if th ... ... pri

Loew's purchase believed possible

By RICHARD G. CASE

Purchase of Loew's Theater in downtown Syracuse by a non-profit citizens group appeared a possibility today.

Fate of the 49-year-old "movie palace" has been in doubt since it was closed last year.

Negotiations have reached the serious point, according to both parties, Sutton Real Estate, owner of the theater and surrounding Loew Building, and Syracuse Area Landmark Theater (SALT), the group founded to save the showplace.

"We're talking," Malcolm Sutton, chairman of realty firm, said today. "Right now, that's all I can say. The conversations are warming up."

Joyce Schriever, SALT chairman, also confirmed the talks but said an agreement had not been reached.

Loew's opened on Salina Street in 1928. Experts consider it one of the last of opulant "movie palaces" built across the country in that period.

It was closed by Loew's Inc. as a film house and legitimate theater in the fall of 1976. Revenue losses were cited.

The Sutton firm, long-time manager of both theater and office building, later purchased the structures but the theater has never reopened.

SALT was formed two years ago to find a way of preserving it.

Mrs. Schriever said the best possibility at the moment appears to be an effort to raise funds to buy Loew's and reopen it, both for films and live theater under a non-profit operation. She noted the success of similar projects in other cities

Herald-Journal, July 7, 1977.

One Step Away

The impasse broke in August, 1977, when Sutton—sympathetic to saving the theater but skeptical of SALT's resources—lowered the price to $65,000, conditional on payment in ninety days. He also assumed the risk of allowing volunteers into the theater for cleaning, repairing, conducting "reacquaintance" tours, and sponsoring events.

Pact Allows SALT To Purchase Loew's

By DOROTHY NEWER

An agreement to purchase Loew's Theater in downtown Syracuse for $65,000 was reached yesterday between Syracuse Area Landmark Theatre Inc. (SALT) and the owner, 362 Salina Street Corp., a company controlled by Sutton Real Estate Co.

Under the terms, SALT, a nonprofit community group, has 90 days to raise the total purchase price but must, within two months, show evidence of having raised $25,000.

SALT was organized to preserve Loew's, one of the plush and gilt movie palaces characteristic of the early 1930s, as a landmark of benefit to downtown following the closing of the theater by the Loew Corp. in 1976. It was purchased, together with the office building, last year by the Suttons.

An early selling price set at $100,000 was reduced to $90,000, according to Malcolm Sutton. This price was further "reduced," he explained, by a $25,000 contribution made by the Sutton company to SALT.

Mrs. Joyce Schrieber, SALT president, said the theater is envisioned as a "cultural center" and also as having revenue-producing use as a place for convention meetings, luncheons, weddings, etc.

The 3,000-seat theater, she said, would supplement the 2,000-seat Civic Center and permit performances and events coming to Syracuse that require houses with larger seating capacity than the Center offers.

The Onondaga County Cultural Resource Council, she pointed out, is represented on the 35-member SALT board, and no conflict is likely to exist with the county facility.

A campaign to raise $100,000, she said, will be designed today on a broad community basis at a SALT meeting. Some of the funds, she said, will be used toward cleaning and getting the building ready for public use.

"I feel it's a sure bet they will meet their goals," Sutton said of SALT's fund-raising plans.

The building, which fronts on S— Street and extends throug— Street, is attached to — Building, which — Street. The t— separated buildi—

As a national landmark, Loew's is eligible for numerous grants, she noted. A $2,500 grant from the state Council for the Arts has already been received for a feasibility study.

Mrs. Schrieber said there has been little vandalism, although some of the theater's seats have been damaged. The art objects in the public rooms, she said, appear to be intact.

Post-Standard, Aug. 13, 1977.

New life for Loew's?
Group has 90 days to raise $65,000

By RICHARD G. CASE

Will the lights go on again behind the darkened marquee of downtown Syracuse's Last Picture Show?

A group of citizens interested in preserving Loew's Theater as a working city center landmark began to struggle with that question yesterday.

Last week they finally reached an agreement putting their money where their thoughts have been during the two years the future of the 49-year-old "movie palace" has been at question.

Syracuse Area Landmark Theatre (SALT) Friday reached a purchase agreement with the owner of Loew's, 362 Salina Street Corp., to buy the closed movie theater wing for $65,000 within 90 days.

If SALT fails, the owners said they will return to their plan to demolish the 3,000-seat theater and turn that section of the Loew Building on Salina Street into a small shopping mall.

What are the prospects?

"We believe Syracuse and Central New York should be able to come through and help us save this magnificent movie palace," said Joyce Schriever, SALT president.

She said the non-profit group wants to

> SALT is looking for donations of time and money to "help save Loew's."
>
> The group has set up a special phone number to receive help from the community: 446-6011.

reopen Loew's as a working theater. To do this, SALT will seek community donations, as well as foundation and other support.

But beyond that buoyant optimism lies the economic reality that Loew's, when it was owned by the movie chain, failed to pay its bills and eventually was closed.

The reality of the downtown market. The reality of new Civic Center, and the War Memorial auditorium, catering to live entertainment and convention needs.

"We won't reopen Loew's as a first-run movie house," SALT lawyer Peter Baum explained. "What we have in mind is to book live entertainment, as well as special films and conventions. We have a lot of ideas."

Among these is understood to be use as a television studio for the newly-chartered cable system in Syracuse; by a community theater group; as the site of specialized film festivals, road shows and benefit programs, as well as an "Entertainment Hall of Fame."

SALT is discussing prospects with the Empire State Theatre and Musical Instrument Museum, now housed at the State Fairgrounds, and the national organization of theater historians.

City Councilor Armond Magnarelli, one of the organizers of SALT, said he feels the theater's lower lobby would be a "good spot" for the cable tv studio and he has discussed the possibility with the firm just awarded the city contract.

Both he and Mrs. Schreiver said they feel there is room for Loew's among Syracuse theaters and the size of the house would give it a booking for certain types of shows.

"I don't feel it would be in competition with the Civic Center," Magnarelli said. "They are pretty well booked."

He said he thought Loew's could offer an advantage of concessions that other theaters, including the Civic Center, do not.

"That's where you make the money," he said. "You give whoever books a show a percentage of the concessions."

Mrs. Schrieber, Magnarelli and others sat down to map the fund-raising campaign yesterday. SALT's president said the group will follow some of the methods used elsewhere to develop a non-profit booking capability.

She cited the examples of Buffalo, Ithaca, Columbus and other cities in which citizen groups were able to buy old theaters closed by the chains and revitalize them.

In Utica, for example, the Central New York Council of the Performing Arts raised $135,000 to buy a Warner Bros. "movie palace," the Stanley, opened in 1927 and designed by the same architect as Loew's, Thomas Lamb. The reopened house is called Stanley Performing Arts Center.

SALT already has a study in hand showing financial possibilities for operating Loew's. It also has grants to support an architectual study.

"The building is in pretty good shape," Mrs. Schriever said. "To reopen on a limited basis, all it needs is a good cleaning. We'd like to try to reopen late next month or in early October."

One of the likely prospects of a revitalized Loew's is cooperation with the city's established community theater, Salt City Playhouse. Playhouse Executive Director Joseph Lotito said yesterday "W— operate in any way pos—

the deeper our involvement the better. We need it."

At present, however, he said this probably would fall short of moving downtown. The playhouse currently rents a former synagogue on University Hill from the city and is proposing to buy the property.

But, Lotito said, "Loew's is a fantastic place for musicals and we do four of those a year. Also for concerts. I think there are a lot of possibilities for expanding our efforts downtown."

Among other possibilities being discussed for Loew's is replacement of the huge theater organ that once was part of the house. (Of the original trappings, only the organ and chandelier were sold by the movie chain before the structure was purchased by Salina Corp.)

Harris Cooper, a SALT board member, said the Loew's organ was sold to a private collector and it is in storage in California. "We might try to get that back or a similiar organ," he explained.

Board members indicated that the immediate goal is to raise the $65,000 purchase price. The owners asked that a "good faith" payment of $1,000 be made Friday and that evidence of at least $25,000 be shown within two months.

Attorney Baum said physical restoration of the house, including replacement of seats, is a long-range goal, to be accomplished gradually. Since Loew's was declared a National Landmark in June, SALT, as owner, would be eligibe for matching federal restoration grants.

Early estimates, Baum said, indicate SALT would be able to operate the theater at a yearly break-even budget of about $162,000, all from rental revenues.

SALT members already are canvassing area groups and promoters to test the level of use if the theater reopened. Baum said an early commitment came from the Syracuse Symphony-Famous Artists series, for six to 10 nights a year.

SALT members plan to use a varie— approaches to fund-raising, from " the theater box office into a large box" to approaching a local far dation or business about the naming the theater in ret— donation that would co— chase.

Loew's, when 1976, was left in do— other, —

L—
to—
a—

Herald-Journal, Aug. 14, 1977.

The Glitter and Glow Returning to Loew's

Post-Standard, Oct. 13, 1977.

By ANITA ALTMAN

There was a time when standard dress at Loew's Theater was sequined gowns, feather boas and long gloves. Against the indescribable background of Persian decor people "used to dress to kill," noted Joanne Nigro, public relations coordinator of the Syracuse Area Landmark Theater, Inc. (SALT) — the non-profit corporation, determined to bring the downtown theater back to life.

In keeping with SALT's goal, the standard garb today is blue jeans and T-shirts as people, instead of dressing to kill, dress to clean.

It's all part of the massive restoration project designed to make Loew's sparkle once more.

Motioning towards two facing chandeliers in the upper lobby of the exquisite theater, Joanne said that the two filigreed brass lamps were the same, although they looked entirely different.

Light glittered through red, blue, green and amber glass panels adding to the mellow quality of the nearest chandelier. The other lamp, at the far end of the corridor, showed no colored panels and only shined dimly through the layers and layers of dust that were yet to be removed.

In May 1975 when Loew's closed for the first time in its 49-year history, the theater was laden with tarnished brass doors, chipped plaster columns, broken stage elevators, dirty red velvet seats, dusty lamps and gummed-up sticky floors.

Harris Cooper, restoration director; and Rick Johnsen, restoration coordinator, found a professional to polish the brass, a master craftsman to fix the plaster, a local expert to repair the elevators and a number of volunteers to wipe off the dust, clean the seats and scrub the floor.

Ed and Dorothy Uhrig along with their sons Eddie and Scott are four of these volunteers.

Every weekend since August, they've come downtown from Baldwinsville to remove the "accumulated years of dirt" from not only the floor, but also from the backs and the bottoms of the seats.

"When the theater opens again, we don't want people to stick to the floors or to the seats," joked Dorothy.

The family's conviction to clean the enticing theater is related to their love for antiques. Although they live in a modern condominium, they often spend their vacations traveling from old estates to sprawling mansions.

"We wanted to become involved in something local that corresponded with our interests," Ed explained.

The Uhrigs found out about the cleaning project from a newspaper advertisement asking for volunteers. "We're not afraid of getting dirty," Dorothy said adding, "But we couldn't get the kids to do this stuff at home."

Yet her sons wouldn't think of spending a weekend without, coming to Loew's. Eddie likes to explore all the beautiful rooms, and sometimes Mom sees Scott just sitting and looking around.

"Everytime you look up, you see something different," Dorothy said.

"Look, there's a mermaid and there's an old man," said Scott, pointing to the carved gold ceiling.

Dorothy piped in, "When you start working in this place, it captures you — you can't let go."

So it doesn't matter if you're listening to a concert or watching a movie or cleaning, Loew's, with all its exotic Oriental splendor, is an experience.

Note: More volunteers are needed to clean Loew's. Just a few hours of your time on the weekends could bring Syracuse's most beautiful theater back to life. Call Rick Johnsen at 446-8484 if you would like to help. Or just show up and tell someone you're there to clean. It's the best investment you could make in downtown Syracuse.

Restoring the Shine

Faithful volunteers who come weekly to help brighten Loew's, four members of the Uhrig family work at cleaning seats. Dorothy and Ed and son Scott are at work, while their other son who shares his father's name gets some pointers from his dad.

55

Volunteers Plunge

Several volunteers remember:

Attorney Peter Baum:

"The breakthrough came when Sutton lowered the price. We had just $2,000, and desperately needed, No. 1, time to raise the funds and, No. 2, access to get the public back into the building. There was concern about security, about liability, about our lack of money for insurance. Harris Cooper [of Cooper Decorations] was of great assistance in negotiating the sale.

"The first thing we had to do was replace about 1,800 lightbulbs—a fraction of what's there. Syroco donated those. A plumbing contractor donated $2,000 worth of services. There are many stories.

"Robert Rodormer [of McAuliffe Paper Co.], who had been president of Edwards Department Store, headed our fund-raising campaign. Volunteers got out solicitation mailings. For ten years Ed and Dorothy Uhrig and their two sons spent most spare moments at the theater. Rick [musical instrument dealer Richard] Johnsen served as volunteer operations manager for ninety days. Volunteers ran tours for hundreds of people.

"I drafted several dozen documents, I guess. From July, 1977, to the end of January, 1978 I probably was spending about twenty-five hours a week on theater business, and I was a sole practitioner with a wife and two children. That made for pretty long days."

Volunteer Dorothy Uhrig:

"Our sons Scott and Ned, then 14 and 16, had never seen the theater, and [husband] Ed and I hadn't for some time. The first day volunteers were allowed in we all went. About ten came. There were no lights.

"The next week we brought our own scrapers and they put in work lights. The only hot water was in the mezzanine men's room. We worked every Saturday. We vacuumed, mopped, and scraped tons of gum off seats and floors. Our refrain was, 'Scrape, scrape, scrape.' We had pizza every night. For awhile our lives revolved around the theater. Once we worked Saturday, Sunday, and Monday getting the theater ready for an opening concert with Harry Chapin."

Senior Technical Engineer Robert Hodge:

"We tried to get enough lighting circuits together for free weekends tours to commence. Whatever we'd touch would short circuit because the old-type insulation used had disintegrated. We replaced the missing Vanderbilt Chandelier with one from the Musicians Gallery, and replaced that with one from behind a pillar. Where glass panels on the marquee were broken, pigeons had got in. We cut new plexiglass panels. The marquee's lower face got new wiring.

"The projection booth [Hodge is a volunteer projectionist] was full of junk. The projectors were operable, but caused print damage. We got a horde of old parts from under the booth. Water pipes [for cooling the projectors] had split. We reestablished a plumbing line.

"Loew's had removed components of the speaker system. We borrowed replacements. We fed many hundreds of feet of new wiring from the stage switchboard. We helped professionals service motors on the stage lift. Volunteers paid for a lot themselves.

"I worked there every weekend for a couple of years. With all due modesty, damn, we were good."

The Landmark Miracle

Near Sutton's deadline, despite its exertions SALT was only halfway to its goal. Then state and federal authorities cooperated in a matching-grant pledge through New York State's parks agency. Sutton extended the purchase deadline, and on June 30, 1978, the theater's ownership passed to SALT. Syracuse's movie palace masterpiece had been saved.

Herald-Journal, October, 1977.

Outside Loew's aid likely

By RICHARD G. CASE

Prospects appeared good today for financial assistance from outside the community in the campaign to buy and restore Loew's Theater.

A citizens group, Syracuse Area Landmark Theatre (SALT), is trying to raise $65,000 within the next two weeks to purchase the downtown landmark from a group of real estate investors and prevent demolition.

SALT reported Monday it has about half of the money in subscriptions and other funds.

At the same time, the group has applied, through the state, for federal assistance in the purchase and a long-term restoration project.

Since Loew's, which opened in 1928, is listed on the National Register of Historic Places, it is eligible for ma... restoration funds.

Indications to... tion may dead...

The visitors will include Fred Rath Jr., deputy state parks commissioner for historic preservation, and his administrative assistant, Mark Lyon.

The visit is being arranged by Laurence D. Martel of Fayetteville, chairman of the Central N w York Park and Recreation Commiss n. It was Martel's interest in the theater project that brought fast action in the usually long application process.

New York State is authorized mo... $1 million in federal preser... tional Park Serv... tional Regi...

In addition, technical assistance of experts could be made available Syracuse group.

"I think it's just a... started," the com... Several year... n...d th...

Post-Standard, Nov. 5, 1977.

Fund Drive Saves Loew's Theater

State Promises $35,000 Boost

The local fund-raising effort to save Loew's theater from the wrecker's ball Friday attracted a promise of state and federal funding that will keep the theater standing.

Frederick L. Rath, state deputy commissioner for historic preservation, said he would recommend the state approve a $35,000 supplement to the funds raised by the nonprofit citizen's group Syracuse Area Landmark Theater Inc. (SALT).

SALT has raised $31,000 toward the theater's purchase price of $65,000.

The extra $1,000 will be a start towards the $35,000 still needed for renovation and operation.

Rath said the recommendation of his department must also receive the approval of the U.S. National Park Service, Department of Interior. The department will supply the funding, he said. He told SALT officials, however, the federal review was "only a formality" following the state's recommendation.

Rath and Lawrence D. Martel, chairman of the Central New York State Park and Recreation Commission, announc the recommendation at a meeting... of SALT attended by loca' and city leaders.

"Here is a structure area whi... th...

roof, recover the seats and repair the stage floor" as first priorities, said Baum.

He said the original $100,000 fund drive was to cover the purchase of the 50-year-old movie palace for $65,000, with the remainder for renovations and to help the theater get financially started.

Baum said the fund drive thus far, coupled with the grant, provides enough to save the building but more is needed to begin operation.

SALT has a nu...er of different fun... raising opera... 'anning s... way o'...

A success! Loew deed to be signed

By RICHARD G. CASE

Legal papers are expected to be signed this week which will seal the success of the two-year campaign to save Loew's Theater.

When the theater was closed in 1976 after nearly 50 years of operation, it was predicted the 3,500-seat "movie palace" in downtown Syracuse would be demolished.

Exchange of deeds this week means the nonprofit citizens group — Syracuse Area Landmark Theater (SALT) — has met the first of several goals in preserving the show place and returning it as a working theater.

The theater wing of the Loew Building on South Salina St. will be sold, under an agreement reached in August of last year, to SALT by the present owner, 362 Salina Street Corp. Principal interest in the firm is held by Sutton Real Estate, which purchased the entire structure from Loew's Corp. in 1976.

$65,000 Grant

Under terms of the purch... cilities in the structur... tained.

This w... anno'

Herald-Journal, June 25, 1978.

The Landmark Challenge

The next hurdle was to staff, operate and restore the theater. SALT converted one volunteer into a paid Operations Manager, hired a young restoration assistant, and others for token pay. The first Executive Director, Rose Bernthal, proved a pivotal, enthusiastic choice. Five-figure grants, from the city, county, New York State, and two regional foundations, helped. Businesses' underwriting of events, volunteers' labor, and individual membership contributions proved crucial.

Rose Bernthal, who with her husband Murray operates Syracuse's Famous Artists agency, recalls:

"The ad hoc committee asked me to come in, to be parttime. I couldn't turn it down. It became fulltime-plus. I had to learn to be a beggar, with my hand out all the time. I arranged to have people on welfare come in and clean. The union agreed not to put in union projectionists. We had wonderful volunteers.

"The people who supported the Landmark Theatre were not rich...not the movers and shakers. It was a 'People's Project.'"

RESTORATION
Gifford Grant Funds Major Restoration of Stage Facilities

Syracuse's Area Landmark Theatre is proud to announce an award of $38,000 by the Rosamond Gifford Charitable Corp. The award, made official by Gifford Executive Director Dean A. Lesinski, has been designated to benefit the extensive upgrading of the Landmark's 50-year-old stage facilities and to allow for the purchase of necessary lighting and sound equipment. According to SALT Board Chairman Peter Baum, "The Gifford aid allows us to begin the first substantial interior restoration of the theatre." Although work has already been completed on a new roof, door repairs and fire escapes, Baum adds, "The key to revitalizing the Landmark lies in our ability to offer modern stage facilities compatible with the requirements of Broadway shows, ballet and major entertainment." Once the work is completed, the Landmark's production potential will be widely enhanced. Already slated for the coming year are two Broadway plays (*Ain't Misbehavin'* and *Showboat*), The Pittsburgh Symphony Orchestra, Folklórica Nacional de Cuba and Le Grand Ballet Canadien.

In addition to these productions, the Gifford aid will enable the Landmark to encourage an extended variety of community presentations. "This is why the Landmark was saved," explains Theatre Director Rose Bernthal. "The Gifford-funded stage renovation becomes an important investment in community interest, giving us the proper facilities to present children's and senior citizens' programs, holiday shows as well as live drama by the theatre-based Landmark Theatre Wing."

Stage improvements to date have included: replacement of the fly system rigging, 75% restoration of the Westinghouse 10-scene switchboard, operational functioning of both stage elevators, orchestra and organ lifts, and partial resurfacing of the stage floor.

back-up drapes and materials required to finish the coating of the stage floor. A hardwood floor since 1928, it will now be covered with a more practical epoxy material, the same used to coat the stages of the new Metropolitan Opera House at Lincoln Center. There will be extensive electrical work, updated to facilitate the requirements of present stage productions. John Seifert, Stage Mangager, adds, "Although the stage is large enough to hold Symphony Orchestras, it was electrically designed for the relatively small demands of vaudeville and simple productions. Lighting and sound amplificiation were primitive compared to what we see today."

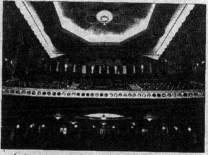

An important acquisition Gifford will provide is the purchase of the Landmark's own stage lighting and sound equipment. Present lighting is marginal, as the Loew's Corp. sold most of its equipment when the theatre switched to an all-movie policy. There has never been a sound system, and high rental costs prevented the theatre from pursuing the number of SALT-sponsored stage productions it would have desired.

Landmark Newsletter, 1979.

Landmark Theatre opens restoration drive

By RICHARD PALMER

A campaign to raise $1.5 million to complete restoration work has been launched by the Syracuse Area Landmark Theatre.

The fund-raiser for the South Salina Street theater was kicked off last week with a $50,000 grant from the Gifford Foundation.

Herald-American photo by Dick Bandy

Rose Bernthal points out features of the Landmark Theater to SALT President Robert Rayback, center, and Francis A. Feil of the Rosamund Gifford Charitable Corp. The Gifford Foundation kicked off new restoration fund drive with a $50,000 contribution.

Plans call for restoration of the former Loew's State Theater to its original 1928 appearance.

SALT President Robert J. Rayback said funds raised thus far have been used to make the structure weatherproof, usable and safe.

'Proved to ourselves'

He said the campaign for full-scale restoration was postponed "until we proved to ourselves and the community the programs the Landmark nurtures and shelters are worthwhile."

The Landmark is one of the few examples of the work of architect Thomas W. Lamb. Its Oriental decor has become famous throughout the country and is included in several theater reference books. It continued as one of several downtown movie theaters until it closed in 1975. The interior had been allowed to deteriorate.

The public realized the city was about to lose a very special asset when the other two major downtown theaters, the Paramount and Keith's, were torn down several years ago to make way for Sibley's. A "Save Loew's" campaign was launched.

Out of the alarm over the loss of the theater with its carved-gilt interior, tapestries and gold leaf trim, a non-profit corporation, SALT, was formed.

National Register

Eventually, the theater was placed on the National Register of Historic Places, and was purchased by SALT.

Since then, more than $300,000

has been spent to make the building functional. Much of the contemplated work will concentrate on the interior cosmetic appearance, according to Rose Bernthal, executive director.

First phase of the new project is to restore the lobbies, including the mezzanine.

Work involves extensive rebuilding and repair of damaged plaster moldings. All ceilings, walls and metal surfaces will be painted and repaired.

Major undertaking

A major undertaking will be the replacement and installation of 13,000 yards of carpeting with padding, at a cost of $54,600.

Several tapestries will be replaced, as well as the addition of a new $34,000 kitchen off the Walnut Room.

Phase 2 calls for repair of damaged plaster, additional repair of ceilings, walls and metal surfaces and damaged gold leaf, an additional 360 yards of tapestry, carpeting the auditorium and balcony isles, repairing, recovering and refinishing seats, and enhancing the sound system.

Phase 3 would see replacement of the heating and cooling plant with energy-saving equipment at a cost of $350,000; installation of an organ, re-acquisition of the Vanderbilt chandelier that hung in the lobby, repair and painting of eight basement rooms and replacement of 220 yards of drapery on the auditorium side aisles.

Don't reflect inflation

Figures were based on estimates made by suppliers in 1980 and 1981 and do not reflect inflation, Mrs. Bernthal said.

Landmark Newsletter, 1979.

RESTORATION

Visitors to the Landmark will likely notice some of the restoration work taking place in preparation for Winter. Under the Salina St. Entrance, the marquee is scraped and ready for new paint as workmen are also busy installing and repairing the bronze doors of Salina and Jefferson Streets. In addition, the Landmark is currently installing new fire escapes in the rear of the building, with work scheduled for completion in the middle of November.

As always, a significant amount of restoration is achieved through the efforts of SALT'S volunteer workers. If you have a special skill or would just like to get involved with this ongoing project, contact Jamie Williams at 475-7723.

Glow of Opulence Returns to Landmark

By CAROL L. BOLL

THE SHOWS AND STARS have come and gone, but 54 years after the opening of Loew's State Theater on S. Salina Street, the real drama is unfolding right in the lobby.

The ornately shaped pillars and bannisters, whose golden luster long ago lost their battle against tarnish, glow with a new brightness. The gargoyle panels above the doorway attract the eye as they probably did that first night in February 1928, when the stage show "Milady's Fan" and the Joan Crawford film "West Point" shared the spotlight with architect Thomas Lamb's opulent architecture for the movie palace's grand opening.

The director of the current drama is Allen Silberman, whose Cortland-based company,

Crown Restoration, has begun what appears to be the mammoth task of restoring the lobby to the same glory that made Loew's State Theater the talk of the town 54 years ago.

The lobby restoration is the high point of an effort that began in 1975, when the theater, victimized by new suburban cinemas and declining city traffic, was scheduled to be demolished and replaced with an office building and parking lot. Syracusans determined to save the landmark from the wrecker's ball banded together to form Syracuse Area Landmark Theater Inc. and eventually purchased the building. About the same time, the theater earned a place on the National Register of Historic Places.

(Continued on Page D-8)

Post-Standard, Nov. 23, 1982.

60

Restoring a Buried Treasure

Allen Silberman pauses, brush in mouth, to survey his handiwork on a bronze panel located over the entrance to the Landmark Theater lobby.

(Concluded from Page D-1)

Since then, the theater — renamed the Landmark — has brought the likes of Andy Williams, Sarah Vaughn, Victor Borge, Rodney Dangerfield and a host of stage and concert attractions to Syracuse.

Restoration has been an ongoing project since the theater was acquired in 1975, but most of the work has been structural repair — on the roof, exit doors, fire escapes, elevators and seat upholstery. The current lobby work, which began last summer and is expected to be completed in February, is the first real "aesthetic restoration effort," according to SALT executive director Rose Bernthal.

The lobby restoration, including new carpeting reweaved in the original pattern, is expected to cost about $60,000, said Bernthal. Much of the money has come from the Rosamond Gifford Charitable Corp. Other contributors include the Central New York Community Foundation and the Landmark Theater Wing Guild.

The theater's listing on the National Register requires that all work on it must exactly duplicate the original work. That includes paint hues, glazes, molding, even the original mistakes, says Silberman.

"Because of the theatrics of it, there are a lot of imperfections in casting," the 39-year-old artist-restorer explained. "You don't want to make it better than it was, so you follow the mistakes. It speaks of the character of the building, the theatrics of it. I mean, this ain't Versailles."

The first step in restoring the lobby involved making a paint analysis on all surfaces to determine their original colors or patterns. In at least one instance, Silberman went through 17 layers of paint before reaching the original shade. He has had to mix most of the new paint himself in order to duplicate the original colors.

Much of the restoration work involves undoing the "improvements" made to the theater in the 1950s. On a wall along the wide staircase, Silberman discovered that a rather flat shade of burgundy paint hid what originally had been a shimmery gold star pattern. In the women's rest room, cotton candy pink on the walls covered a walnut veneer with hand-carved accents.

One of the most striking changes can be seen on the Indo-Persian pillars, which also fell victim to the good intentions of a previous owner who attempted to spruce them up with bright red, blue and gold paint.

Silberman and his two-man crew of Glen Hinchey and Steve Thane have covered the bright paint with tissue-thin sheets of silver leafing. The sheets are gently pressed over the surfaces of the ornate pillars and then covered with a thin layer of gold glaze and touches of red and green glazes. The finished effect is a gold pillar with a translucent sheen and just enough muted color to call attention to the intricate relief pattern.

"The hardest part of it is to get the right look," Silberman said of the gold tone, he is trying to bring out. "We want to do it so that it does not look brand new, but looks well taken care of. It should look about five years old. ... It was never bright, bright shiny.",

A former student of anthropology and a self-described "closet archaeologist," Silberman has gone back to architect Lamb's and owner Marcus Loew's own concept of the building in his effort to bring out its original character.

Landmark Theatre given $75,000

Gifford Foundation funds will help ongoing renovation

By Bob Curley
Staff Writer

The Landmark Theatre is renowned as a plush 1928 Indo-Persian movie palace that transports its patrons into an exciting fantasyland.

However, it has always been especially exciting, even scary, for people in wheelchairs, who have to be hand-carried to bathrooms that are up or down long flights of stairs.

Now, thanks to a $75,000 grant from the Rosamond Gifford Charitable Corporation, the theater management hopes to introduce a modern innovation — an elevator.

The announcement was made by Rose Bernthal, Landmark director, who praised the Gifford Foundation for the new gift and for an earlier grant of $50,000 that provided more than one-half of the cost of new carpeting and restoration of the grand foyer and the promenade lobby.

"An elevator will cost about $100,000. Although we do not have all the money," she said, has been spent refurbishing lobbies and dressing rooms, restoring the marquee and outer doors, repairing the roof, installing security doors, and providing an emergency lighting system.

In April the venerable showplace received a grant of $150,000 from the National Heritage Trust, a public benefit corporation established in 1968 by the New York State Legislature. Much of that grant is directed toward seat restoration, and work is scheduled to begin in January when there is less activity in the theater. Other funds will be used to improve electrical capacity and safety for both the stage and auditorium.

"We still have a long way to go — even though we've entertained more than 3½ million people since the reopening in 1977. The seats are in deplorable condition; the tapestries are torn; much of the gold leaf is missing; and there is a desperate need for the elevator for the handicapped and the elderly," Bernthal said.

"We now have 27 business and community leaders serving

Herald-American, Nov. 10, 1985.

It's standing room only at Landmark Theatre

With the seats out of the Landmark Theatre, workers have plenty of room for cleaning and other work.

Post-Standard, Feb. 13, 1986.

Landmark Theatre Newsletter, Feb.-Mar., 1983.

Restoration News Update

The restoration of the Landmark's main lobby is continuing smoothly with the repainting of the intricate and colorful patterns on the ceiling domes which hover over the chandeliers. Allen Silberman, director of Crown Restoration, is restoring the domes with the assistance of Steve Thane, using some stenciling methods, but most of the work is done free-hand. Allen expects to have both domes completed by the end of March.

At this very moment, Bloomsburg Carpet Industries are weaving the carpeting which will be ready & installed sometime in March. Samples of the original carpet in the 2 different patterns were sent to them and the Salina Street Lobby, Grand Staircase and Grand Promenade will now be beautiful underfoot as well as above.

Speaking of carpeting, the Walnut Room in the lower level of the Theatre was recently spruced up with gold wall-to-wall carpeting donated by the management of Syracuse Mall. The carpeting was removed from the old Mall building at Clinton Square by Ron Squires, Operations Director at the Landmark, and a crew of volunteers. Although the carpeting is not matched to the original, it will serve as a functional, temporary replacement until funds are raised for new original-pattern carpeting.

In the meantime, the gold carpeting gives the room wonderful acoustics and a luxurious appearance.

Presently being rewired by Mark Wroblewski, the Landmark's State Manager, the Walnut Room will be available in a short time to rent for private and public events. Inquiries for rental of any part of the Theatre may be made by calling Rose Bernthal, Executive Director, at 475-7979.

Please come down & see the gorgeous work that has been done. Our members have been so loyal to the Landmark that it gives us real pleasure to have you see the theatre shine from your support.

What's Been Done

Purchased Building Outright......$65,000

Renovated Outer Proscenium

    Window....................................15,000

Repointed Exterior Masonry.........22,000

Repaired Auditorium Roof...........88,000

Restored Bronze Entrance Doors

    to both Street Lobbies...............27,000

New Stage Draperies..................15,000

New Stage Lighting and

    Sound System...........................23,000

Restored Sprinkler below Stage

    and Entire Fire Hose System........9,000

Rebuilt Fire Escapes....................21,000

Repaired Auditorium Exit Doors

    to Code.....................................8,000

Improved Air Conditioning............7,000

Made All Plumbing Operational...15,000

Devoted Volunteers Have Contributed Tens of Thousands of Hours to Restoration and have:

-Cleaned entire interior including removal of 700 lbs of gum

-Repointed, gilded, and painted entrances, including trim, display cases and marquee ceiling

-Restored original switchboard for stage and auditorium lighting

Landmark Legend newsletter, Jan./Feb./Mar., 1997.

Saving the building was easy:
All it took was love and hard work

"The volunteers have been invaluable over the years," said board president Ron Engan. "We use them for ushers, for cleanup, and also for renovation. We have called on the volunteers constantly."

"Give all kinds of kudos to the volunteers," said Rose Bernthal, who was the theater's executive director for eight years. "They have been the core and the soul of that place. Whenever something was needed, we could turn to them, and we did. We could never have done it without them.

"And the staff too — they've always been poorly paid and very devoted. They, and the volunteers, have been marvelous to that theater. They've kept it alive."

When asked why they have donated hundreds of hours, buckets of sweat and elbow grease and bales of energy this last decade to keep a gaudy, gilt-covered plaster-and-velvet palace of make believe from self-destructing, most of the volunteers say, "I don't know."

But if you keep them talking, some rea-

sons take shape.

For the Uhrigs, working at the Landmark has been something they could do together as a family, just as camping has been. Both of their sons have grown up there, learned there, and worked there. Scott, 24, is now the Landmark's house electrician; Ed, 26, has worked as a bartender there, and became interested in locksmithing, which is what he now does for a living, through the volunteers he worked with.

For Robert Hodge, an engineer in the

★ VOLUNTEERS, Page 5

★ VOLUNTEERS
Continued from Page 3
audio visual department at Syracuse University's Newhouse School of Communication, what started out as the challenge of rebuilding the theater's 40-year-old projectors evolved into something deeper.

"I wish I could be more philosophical about it, because in a way, that's what it is, a philosophy. It is a belief that, as a building, as a form, this is something that will never, ever be capable of being replaced. It's also a belief that, since the Landmark is the last of its type in the city, it deserves the recognition I've given it over the years. It just seemed like the proper thing to do."

Hodge's recognition has translated into countless hours spent scavenging, rebuilding and running the theater's three 35-millimeter film projectors and its antiquated sound system, as well as countless other hours "pulling miles and miles of wire, fixing seats and pipes, reworking chandeliers, and doing "virtually anything that was necessary."

All of the volunteers spoke of the need to save the Landmark for the community, for its architectural value, for its beauty, and because it is the last of the great Salina Street theaters.

"I like an old theater, I like old restored buildings," said Bob Reep, who has spent nine years of Saturdays painting walls and climbing ladders to dab paint onto telltale white spots where the theater's plaster shows through. "It's the style. You just don't see the style anymore. The modern is just not as grand. Look at this," he says, gesturing at the theater's ornate lobby. "You'll never see it again. No one can afford it."

To a person, the volunteers all downplay their individual efforts on behalf of the Landmark, and all mention the names of at least one or two they say have done as much or more.

They are uncomfortable talk-

Herald-American, Nov. 8, 1987.

Stuffing envelopes at the Landmark are, from left: Marla Reep of Clay, and Dorothy and Ed Uhrig of Baldwinsville.

Herald-American, Nov. 8, 1987.

After eighteen years of painting, volunteer Robert Reep recalls:

"In 1978 my wife and I went to a Tommy Dorsey concert at the Landmark and saw [director] Rose Bernthal. She said she was looking for volunteers to help restore the theater. I started out helping reupholster seats. I was Budget Director for the Department of Agriculture Soil Conservation Service and had never done that kind of work. But I learned.

"Then I got to painting downstairs. Several of us patched big holes where water had come in. At first I brought my own tools and lights. Later they got a floodlight.

"I just kept coming, on most Saturdays, Sundays, and holidays, for eighteen years. I've painted the the stage, the hallway, lobby, and mezzanine trim, and all around the auditorium. I bought all my own brushes—I'd say at least a hundred.

"For awhile there were volunteers every-

where, trying to get the water going, for electrical work, you name it. Many times I'd tell my wife, 'I'm going now. If I'm not back, you know where I am.'

"The thing is, you'd go in the back door, there'd be no light but one floodlight in the upper-balcony. You didn't know if anybody was there, from the last show or anything. It was real frightening.

"One time I re ember going into the basement Screening Room, because that's where they were storing parts. I opened the door and a cold draft rushed out. I looked down and saw a shadow with a hand out with a sword. It scared the heck out of me —it was a prop.

"One Sunday I went in and heard a drip, drip, drip. A hose to the water-cooled projectors was broken. A lot of times I think we saved real damages."

Anniversaries Accumulate

In its first autumn of ownership SALT instituted a precedent of anniversary fund-raisers—which remain essential to theater restoration. This gala was enriched by the spirit, though not persona, of comedian George Burns.

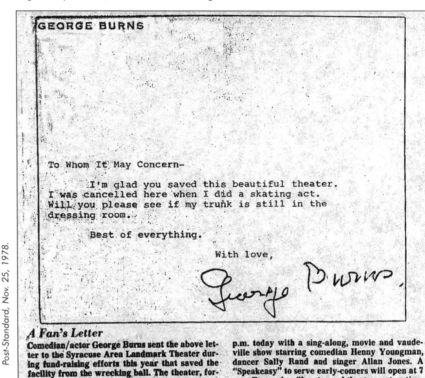

Post-Standard, Nov. 25, 1978.

GEORGE BURNS

To Whom It May Concern—

I'm glad you saved this beautiful theater. I was cancelled here when I did a skating act. Will you please see if my trunk is still in the dressing room.

Best of everything.

With love,

George Burns.

A Fan's Letter

Comedian/actor George Burns sent the above letter to the Syracuse Area Landmark Theater during fund-raising efforts this year that saved the facility from the wrecking ball. The theater, formerly Loew's, will mark its 50th anniversary at 8 p.m. today with a sing-along, movie and vaudeville show starring comedian Henny Youngman, dancer Sally Rand and singer Allan Jones. A "Speakeasy" to serve early-comers will open at 7 p.m. Proceeds will go toward theater restoration.

Landmark gala attracts 2,500

By ANDREW RESCHKE
(Other picture on Page One)

The marquee was lit up with the names of the headliners for the vaudeville show. Outside were nearly a dozen classic automobiles. Inside, scattered in the crowd were men dressed in white tie and tails and women in the finest fashions of the Twenties.

You'd have thought it was the grand opening of a new theater downtown in the Flapper era. What it was, however, was the gala celebrating the 50th anniversary of the show palace now known as the Landmark Theater, formerly Loew's State.

A near-sellout crowd of more than 2,500 patrons attended the event last night. Everyone was invited to wear Twenties-style dress, and a surprisingly large number chose to do so. Members of the staff, were of course decked out in such styles, but there also were numerous others who elected to wear the Twenties garb, and it made the occasion all the more festive.

It has been amazing what the members of SALT have been able to accomplish with the old theater in just one year. And, she never looked better than she did last night.

Both the upstairs and downstairs lobbies were opened to the public, and many who attended the affair last night arrived early to tour the renovated masterpiece of theater architecture.

Decorating the theater was the furniture which had been bought and placed in the theater from 11 countries 50 years ago. The fountain upstairs also was working.

In addition, several bars were set up throughout the lobbies to refresh the patrons. Also, there were exhibits of movie ads, programs and old photographs of shows from the heyday of live entertainment at Loew's State.

In keeping with the theme of the Twenties, both films and a vaudeville show were presented on the bill. A console organ and an orchestra were present to make the event even more authentic.

The program began with Donald Scott at the organ, playing various selections while late-comers made their way to their seats.

The majority of what was offered weren't really movies, but rather short advertisements for various products and causes. Drawing laughter and calling up memories for many in attendance were ads for the theater's 1954 Academy Award contest; a WHEN-TV ad promoting the showing of M-G-M films on that station when it was known as Channel 8; a commercial for a paint store, and even a commercial pushing dinnerware known as "beetleware," which was given away free once a week.

A preview of the film "Gone with the Wind" found members of the audience applauding their favorite stars from that classic. And classic is the word to describe a clip showing Eddie Cantor drumming up support for an unemployed benefit which was to be held back in the Thirties.

These were followed by a Movietone newsreel, with veteran Lowell Thomas reporting on Franklin Roosevelt's construction of his home in Hyde Park and China's struggle with Japan prior to World War II.

The film sequences concluded with the showing of a part of the film, "The Further Perils of Laurel and Hardy."

Donald Scott returned to the organ to accompany the audience in what was obviously their favorite part of the festivities, a sing-along.

The gala's master of ceremonies, Armond Magnarelli, came on stage after intermission, and introduced Carl Silfer and the orchestra, which presented a short overture, before the vaudeville portion of the evening began.

This was followed by a demonstration of precision line dancing by Jack Gronau and his Dance Unlimited troupe. They tapped to the tune of "Tea for Two" and "I Wanna Be Happy."

Next on the bill came the animal act, a fixture in any vaudeville show. Last night's act was the Burger Animal Review, and they impressed with their skill and ability. Included in the review were a pony, chimp, and numerous dogs, featuring the only performing Afgans in show business.

Allan Jones was the first of the show's three headliners to make his appearance. Jones, a remarkably youthful 71, opened his stint with renditions of "With a Song In My Heart," David Gates' "If" and Jacques Brel's "Amsterdam."

Herald-American, Nov. 26, 1978.

Landmark turns 70 amid many memories

▶ The theater's past is honored at a anniversary gala.

By Charles D. Jackson
Staff Writer

Rep. James Walsh remembers seeing a lot of movies in the Landmark Theatre as a little boy.

"My uncle, who was a police officer at the time, used to sneak me and a bunch of other kids in through the side door," Walsh recalled while attending a special 70th Anniversary Gala for the Landmark Theatre Wednesday night.

Walsh said he has gone to movies and concerts at the theater for the past 40 years.

"I've seen Dylan here, the Byrds, and 10 years ago, I took my daughter to see a young woman who was a heartthrob back then — Debbie Gibson."

Walsh added that he has enjoyed being a part of the theater's success, especially during the mid-'70s, when the theater's destiny was almost wrapped up in a wrecking ball.

"Being involved in government, it was a pleasure to have worked with Rose Bernthal and (then-executive director) Frank Malfitano to help get city funds and come up with a good tax agreement. The fact that the community pulled together then and are still working together now says a lot."

The theater opened Feb. 18, 1928, as Loew's State Theatre. It came close to being razed in the mid-1970s, years after it was abandoned as a movie theater by the Loew's operation. A group of local people bought the theater in 1976.

Walsh was one of about 250 people who attended the event, which

BILL KNOWLTON, center, the Landmark Theatre's historian and a charter board member, gives a tour

PETER CHEN/Staff photographer

of the theater Wednesday night during its 70th anniversary celebration.

was also a fund-raiser for the theater.

The celebration included a tour, food and wine samples from area merchants, and a silent auction for the theater's memorabilia. Some of the items included a songbook signed by singer Luther Vandross, a playbill signed by singer Lena Horne and a hat signed by the Dave Matthews band.

The 1928 Greta Garbo silent movie "Love" was shown during the bash. It was the second film screened in Loew's State Theatre.

For Sally Yarwood, the celebration marked two birthdays for

her. "I just turned 70 in September, and here we are celebrating the 70th birthday of this beautiful theater. I grew up with this theater."

Yarwood, who has been ushering at the theater for the past 25 years, said she remembers the organ that used to be in the theater, and which was used to accompany silent movies.

"I never saw the silent movies, but I remember coming to other shows over the years and seeing the same organ they used." She said one of the many shows she recalled enjoying was a Diana Ross concert in the '70s.

"This is a one-of-a-kind theater; there's nothing like it in this area. I hope it stays around another 70 years."

Michael Loguidice, chairman of the Landmark Theatre Board of Trustees, used the event as a platform to announce the naming of the theater's new manager, Dennis Snow, a local business owner and former director of the War Memorial.

Snow, who grew up in Syracuse, recalled his most memorable Landmark Theatre moment.

"I first came here as a little boy to see 'Frankenstein.' It scared the hell out of me."

Herald-Journal, Feb. 19, 1998

67

Events, Events, Events

From blues, country music, and rock to ballet, plays, movies, and standup comedy, The Landmark has presented the most diverse entertainment of any Syracuse venue. Though the theater has no risk capital for its own productions, event-presenters consider its size and splendor a unique combination. A sampling of its own and others' presentations:

CASINO NIGHT
Gala fundraiser kicks off Fall 1979

September 15 promises to be an exciting night in Syracuse! The event is the Landmark's first annual Casino Night, bringing international fun and glamour to the ornate lobbies of downtown's only "Palace." Set as a fundraiser for the theatre restoration, festivities will begin at 9 p.m., as guests are invited to enjoy champagne, hors d'œuvres, dancing, and very special live music by the Tommy Smith Trio.

Naturally, the highlight of the evening will be Monte Carlo-style gambling with the opportunity and challenge of five different games of chance. Included will be Blackjack, Big Six, Roulette, and the Money Wheel—all the ingredients of an unforgettable evenings.

Continuing until 1 a.m., tickets for Landmark Theatre Casino Night are $10 per person and are tax-deductible contributions to the restoration fund. For reservations and more information, call the Box Office at 475-7980. We hope to see you!

Newsletter, Fall, 1979. Landmark Theatre Archive.

SLY FOX

Friday and Saturday
February 1 & 2, 8 and 9
8:00
Saturday February 16
4:30 and 8:00

Produced by our own Landmark Theatre Wing Sly Fox involves the crafty antics of a wealthy man in the early 1900's who pretends to be dying for the sole purpose of soliciting gifts from equally greedy friends wishing to become his sole heir.
For tickets call the Landmark 475-7980.

JERRY GARCIA

Tuesday February 19, 8:00
For tickets, Call the Landmark 475-7980

GLENN MILLER ORCHESTRA CONCERT

Wednesday, February 27, 8:00pm

The big bands are back and the Landmark is pleased to announce a special concert by The World Famous Glenn Miller Orchestra.
Sponsored by the Crouse-Hinds Company, the concert will benefit the Syracuse YMCA.
Tickets are $10 and $8, but may be purchased for $8 and $6 at any Fay's Drug Store.
The Glenn Miller Orchestra, directed by Jimmy Henderson with the Moonlight Serenaders, is the only authentic Glenn Miller Orchestra legally authorized to carry the name of the famous bandleader of the early forties.
Tickets are available at the Landmark Theatre Ticket Office, the Downtown YMCA, 340 Montgomery Street, the North Area Family YMCA at 4775 Wetzel Road, Liverpool, as well as all Fay's Drug Stores.

ALVIN AILEY
Repertory Ensemble

Thursday, February 28, 8:30pm

Syracuse University Union Performing Arts Board, in association with Columbia Artists will present the return engagement of the Alvin Ailey Repertory Ensemble. This group of young dancers has developed under the aegis of the famed Alvin Ailey American Dance Theater. The group is composed mainly of students from the Ailey School and they have been drawing both critical and audience acclaim for performances in the U.S.
Tickets may be obtained by calling 423-2503.

"Ain't Misbehavin"

Sunday, March 2,

Monday, March 3, 8:30pm

What more can be said about the breathtaking, super song and dance musical "Ain't Misbehavin"? It's taken Broadway by storm, playing to roaring, stomping, SRO audiences every night.
You'll be tapping your toes and singing the praises of Fats Waller's inimitable music as it takes you through the 20's, 30's and 40's in a whirlwind of sight and sound. Don't miss it! Tickets may be obtained by calling 424-8210.

ANDRE PREVIN And The Pittsburgh Symphony

Wednesday, March 5, 8:30pm

Without a doubt one of the half-dozen greatest orchestras today, the Pittsburgh Symphony achieves new levels of virtuosity under the baton of charismatic Andre Previn. Syracuse is one of the few cities lucky enough to schedule a date with this magnificent ensemble.
Tickets may be obtained by calling 424-8210.

FOLKLORICO NACIONAL de CUBA

Friday, March 7, 8:30pm

One of the most impressive attractions of the year — a whirling, swirling explosion of color and excitement. Unbelievable athleticism with irresistible Afro-Cuban rhythms. The Folklorico at last brings the unsurpassed vitality and consummate artistry of Cuba to the world.
Tickets may be obtained by calling 424-8210.

HIGH LIGHTS

Young People And Restoration At SALT

The Landmark Theatre is now an agency for the Syracuse University Work Study program and three architecture students are now assisting Jamie Williams in his efforts as the SALT Restoration Assistant.
Through the S.U. Community Internship Program, SALT benefits from the work of a student photographer and another architecture student.
The Manpower division of Onondaga County will subsidize the employment of five young workers and a supervisor to assist the restoration effort. The Youth Community Conservation Improvement Project grant has been approved. Jamie Williams is now interviewing prospective workers and the theatre is also seeking a qualified supervisor.

Newsletter, February, 1980. Landmark Theatre Archive.

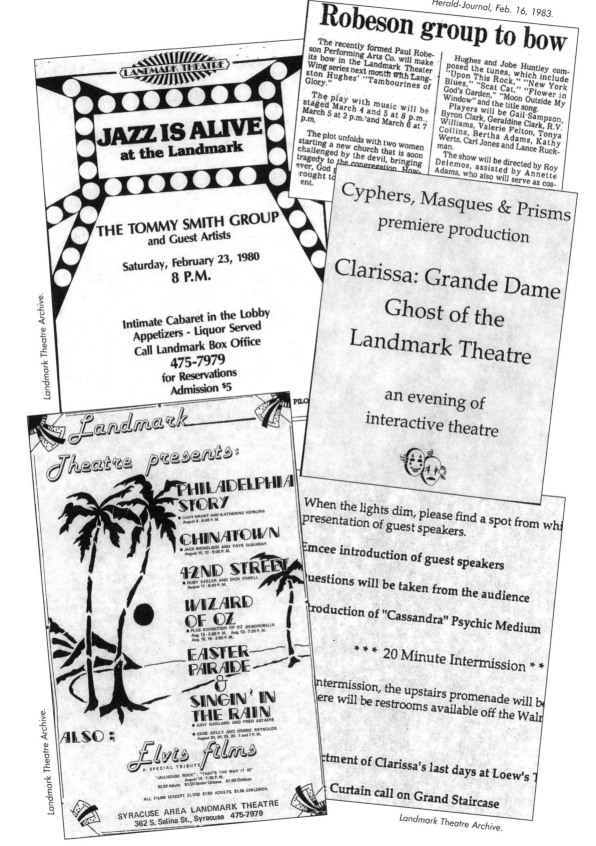

LANDMARK THEATRE

JAZZ IS ALIVE
at the Landmark

THE TOMMY SMITH GROUP
and Guest Artists

Saturday, February 23, 1980
8 P.M.

Intimate Cabaret in the Lobby
Appetizers - Liquor Served
Call Landmark Box Office
475-7979
for Reservations
Admission $5

Herald-Journal, Feb. 16, 1983.

Robeson group to bow

The recently formed Paul Robeson Performing Arts Co. will make its bow in the Landmark Theater Wing series next month with Langston Hughes' "Tambourines of Glory."

The play with music will be staged March 4 and 5 at 8 p.m., March 5 at 2 p.m. and March 6 at 7 p.m.

The plot unfolds with two women starting a new church that is soon challenged by the devil, bringing tragedy to the congregation. However, God p[...] rought to [...] ent.

Hughes and Jobe Huntley composed the tunes, which include "Upon This Rock," "New York Blues," "Scat Cat," "Flower in God's Garden," "Moon Outside My Window" and the title song.

Players will be Gail-Sampson, Byron Clark, Geraldine Clark, R.V. Williams, Valerie Felton, Tonya Collins, Bertha Adams, Kathy Werts, Carl Jones and Lance Ruckman.

The show will be directed by Roy Delemos, assisted by Annette Adams, who also will serve as cos-[...]

Cyphers, Masques & Prisms
premiere production

Clarissa: Grande Dame
Ghost of the
Landmark Theatre

an evening of
interactive theatre

Landmark
Theatre presents:

PHILADELPHIA STORY
CARY GRANT AND KATHERINE HEPBURN
August 3 - 8:00 P. M.

CHINATOWN
JACK NICHOLSON AND FAYE DUNAWAY
August 10, 12 - 8:00 P. M.

42ND STREET
RUBY KEELER AND DICK POWELL
August 17 - 8:00 P.M.

WIZARD OF OZ
PLUS EXHIBITION OF OZ MEMORABILIA
Aug. 12 - 2:00 P. M.   Aug. 13 - 7:30 P. M.
Aug. 16, 16 - 2:00 P. M.

EASTER PARADE &
SINGIN' IN THE RAIN
JUDY GARLAND AND FRED ASTAIRE
GENE KELLY AND DEBBIE REYNOLDS
August 23, 24, 25, 26 - 1 and 7 P.M.

ALSO:

Elvis films
A SPECIAL TRIBUTE
"JAILHOUSE ROCK" "THAT'S THE WAY IT IS"
August 19 - 7:30 P. M.
$2.50 Adults $1.50 Senior Citizens $1.00 Children
ALL FILMS (EXCEPT ELVIS) $1.50 ADULTS, $1.00 CHILDREN

SYRACUSE AREA LANDMARK THEATRE
362 S. Salina St., Syracuse 475-7979

When the lights dim, please find a spot from whi[...]
presentation of guest speakers.

Emcee introduction of guest speakers

Questions will be taken from the audience

Introduction of "Cassandra" Psychic Medium

*** 20 Minute Intermission **

[...]ntermission, the upstairs promenade will b[...]
[...]ere will be restrooms available off the Waln[...]

[...]ctment of Clarissa's last days at Loew's T[...]

[...] Curtain call on Grand Staircase

3rd Annual
Halloween at the Landmark

Storytelling by
Childrens Author
Bruce Coville

Theatrically Illustrated by
Open Hand Theatre

Haunted House
in "Catacombs" of the Landmark
(created by Nottingham High School
Meadowbrook Harlequins)

Friday, October 24, 6 and 8 p[...]

Saturday, October 25, 1, 3, 6, 8 [...]

NUTCRACKER
MOSCOW STATE BALLET
MOSCOW STATE ORCHESTRA
of the Natalia Sats Theatre

Direct from Russia!
4 Christmas Spectacular!

SYRACUSE, NY
LANDMARK THEATRE
DECEMBER 14 & 15

Sponsored By

EMBASSY SUITES HOTEL · FOX 68 WSYT

Y94FM · A Dickens Christmas

TAMMY WYNETTE
The First Lady of Country Music
IN CONCERT

2 time Grammy Award winner
☆ Over 35 #1 hits
   ☆ Biggest selling single in country
      music history "Stand By Your Man"

**Friday, March 30th
Syracuse Landmark Theater**

Andre Previn and
PITTSBURGH
SYMPHONY

LANDMARK THEATRE WED., MARCH 5 - 8:30
$12.50, $11.50, $10.50, $9.00   424-8210
SYRACUSE SYMPHONY FAMOUS ARTISTS

Landmark Theatre Archive.

Programs also include "The Walk of Stars" and "Landmark Theatre Award of Excellence," both originated by SALT; the recording industry's annual regional "Sammy Awards"; and twice weekly midday "walkup" tours, plus (by reservation only) "any-day" tours for groups, conducted by volunteers.

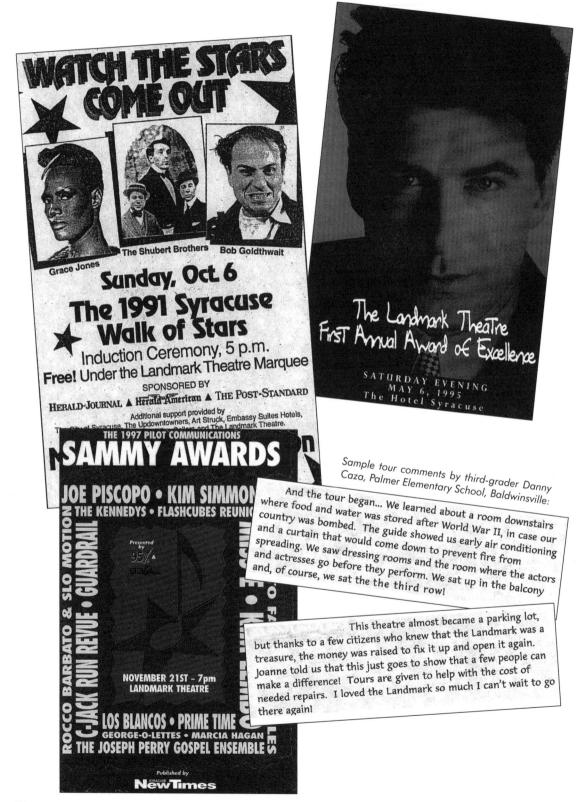

WATCH THE STARS COME OUT

Grace Jones   The Shubert Brothers   Bob Goldthwait

Sunday, Oct. 6
The 1991 Syracuse
Walk of Stars
Induction Ceremony, 5 p.m.
Free! Under the Landmark Theatre Marquee

SPONSORED BY
HERALD-JOURNAL ▲ Herald-American ▲ THE POST-STANDARD

Additional support provided by
The City of Syracuse, The Updowntowners, Art Struck, Embassy Suites Hotels, ... and The Landmark Theatre.

The Landmark Theatre
First Annual Award of Excellence

SATURDAY EVENING
MAY 6, 1995
The Hotel Syracuse

THE 1997 PILOT COMMUNICATIONS
SAMMY AWARDS

JOE PISCOPO • KIM SIMMON
THE KENNEDYS • FLASHCUBES REUNIO

ROCCO BARBATO & SLO MOTION
C-JACK RUN REVUE • GUARDRAIL

Presented by
95X & 93Q

NOVEMBER 21ST ~ 7pm
LANDMARK THEATRE

LOS BLANCOS • PRIME TIME
GEORGE-O-LETTES • MARCIA HAGAN
THE JOSEPH PERRY GOSPEL ENSEMBLE

Published by
SYRACUSE
NewTimes

Sample tour comments by third-grader Danny Caza, Palmer Elementary School, Baldwinsville:

And the tour began... We learned about a room downstairs where food and water was stored after World War II, in case our country was bombed. The guide showed us early air conditioning and a curtain that would come down to prevent fire from spreading. We saw dressing rooms and the room where the actors and actresses go before they perform. We sat up in the balcony and, of course, we sat the the third row!

This theatre almost became a parking lot, but thanks to a few citizens who knew that the Landmark was a treasure, the money was raised to fix it up and open it again. Joanne told us that this just goes to show that a few people can make a difference! Tours are given to help with the cost of needed repairs. I loved the Landmark so much I can't wait to go there again!

Stars Who Have Graced the Theater's Stage

(partial list)

Larry Adler
Morey Amsterdam
Phil Baker
Count Basie
Harry Belafonte
Tony Bennett
Jack Benny
Milton Berle
Ben Blue
Victor Borge
Cab Calloway
George Carlin
The Carter Family
Johnny Cash
Ray Charles
Van Cliburn
Natalie Cole
Judy Collins
Perry Como
Harry Connick, Jr.
Bill Cosby
Rodney Dangerfield
Miles Davis
Vilma and Buddy Ebsen
Billy Eckstine
Les and Larry Elgart
Gloria Estefan
Roberta Flack
Henry Fonda
Arlo Guthrie
Jean Harlow
Horace Heidt
Lou Holtz
Lena Horne
Englebert Humperdinck
The Ink Spots
B.B. King
Jay Leno
Ted Lewis
Leo the Lion
Barry Manilow

Marcel Marceau
Wynton Marsalis
Johnny Mathis
Butterfly McQueen
Robert Merrill
Bill Monroe
Moscow Ballet
Nana Mouskouri
Willie Nelson
Peter Nero
Wayne Newton
New York City Opera
Rudolf Nureyev
Luciano Pavarotti
Gregory Peck
Joe Penner
Peter, Paul, and Mary
Pittsburgh Symphony
Leontyne Price
John Raitt
Sally Rand
Debbie Reynolds
The Ritz Brothers
Joan Rivers
Kenny Rogers
Mickey Rooney
Mark Russell
Roxy's Gang
Pete Seeger
Jerry Seinfeld
Ricky Skaggs
Bruce Springsteen
Joan Sutherland
The Three Stooges
Sophie Tucker
Bobby Vinton
Waring's Pennsylvanians
Andy Williams
Tammy Wynette
Henny Youngman

(Plus numerous others for the Walk of Stars, Sammy Awards, Syracuse Symphony. Syracuse Opera, and in touring musicals.)

The Landmark's Fame

One measure of the theater's significance is coverage in books, magazines, movies, videos, and museum exhibitions about movie palaces. A sampling:

GREAT AMERICAN CINEMAS

THE SYRACUSE AREA LANDMARK THEATRE

Syracuse, New York

The Syracuse Area Landmark Theatre in Syracuse, New York, provides a forum as magnificent as the films it was meant to showcase. The theater's opulent interior transported Depression-era patrons from their work-a-day world to the glitter and glamour of Hollywood, and today, continues its tradition of grand entertainment in a grand setting.

The theater was designed by architect Thomas W. Lamb and was christened Loew's State Theatre on February 18, 1928. Built at the close of the Roaring Twenties, Loew's State offered freewheeling audiences double bills of famous stage acts and first-run moving pictures. When the stock market crashed a year later, patrons continued to flock to the theater, where grandeur replaced despair.

The theater provided the ultimate escape. Often labeled Indo-Persian, architect Lamb further described the theater as "European, Byzantine, Romanesque — which is the Orient as it came to us through the merchants of Venice."

Audiences were ushered into Lamb's exotic world through the main lobby, which boasted a chandelier designed by Louis Tiffany for Cornelius Vanderbilt's mansion, and the grandest of the theater's several huge murals. The Musician's Gallery, located over the front doors, featured quartet serenades as intermission entertainment during the '30s. Patrons who ascended the grand staircase reached the promenade lobby, where they delighted in finding a fish pond with a Japanese pagoda fountain. The main auditorium, which houses 1,832 of the theater's 3,300 seats, was decorated in rich reds and golds and accented with wall ornaments throughout. The 1,400-pipe Wurlitzer organ offered its own exotic flavor, treating patrons to such sounds as a glockenspiel, marimba, bird whistles, hoof beats and surf sounds.

Crowds flocked to Loew's State throughout the Depression and World War II and yet, like so many other great movie palaces (including six razed in Syracuse), the theater's attendance began dropping steadily in the '50s. By 1975, it seemed that the pride of Syracuse would fall prey to the wrecker's ball to allow for a parking/shopping complex. However, in 1977, a group of concerned citizens banded together to form the Syracuse Area Landmark Theatre, or SALT. SALT had the local landmark placed on the National Register of Historic Places, opening the door to government funding.

By the end of 1977, the group had acquired the theater and begun restoring its original splendor. Impressed with the dedication of the SALT volunteers and staff, New York State's Parks Commission began offering ongoing funding, as have Onondaga County and the City of Syracuse. Today, the theater continues its restoration and fund-raising efforts, while offering the Syracuse area a full schedule of live performances by the Syracuse Symphony, touring Broadway shows and a wide variety of renowned musicians.
—B.A.R.

American Movie Classics Magazine, March, 1991.

The Louis XVI and Italian Baroque designs soon led Lamb into more and more flamboyant experiments until, near the end of the Twenties, he had thrown purism to the winds in favor of Hindu, Chinese, Persian, Spanish, and Romanesque themes. An interesting illustration of this new mood was a series of theatres designed for the Loew chain. Loew's State in Syracuse, New York, was the prototype of three Oriental extravaganzas that made his early Adam efforts look like Quaker meetinghouses. The Syracuse theatre was opened in 1929, Loew's 175th Street Theatre in New York in 1930, and Loew's 72nd Street

"The Grand Foyer," wrote Lamb, in describing the theatre in Syracuse, "is like a temple of gold set with colored jewels, the largest and most precious of which is a sumptuous mural. It represents a festive procession all in Oriental splendor, with elephants, horses, slaves, princes and horsemen, all silhouetted against a deep-blue night sky. It is pageantry in its most elaborate form, and immediately casts a spell of the mysterious and, to the Occidental mind, of the exceptional. Passing on into the inner foyers and the mezzanine promenade, one continues in the same Indo-Persian style with elaborate ornamentation both in relief and in painting, all conspiring to create an effect thoroughly foreign to our Western minds. These exotic ornaments, colors, and scenes are particularly effective in creating an atmosphere in which the mind is free to frolic and becomes receptive to entertainment.

"The auditorium itself is also very much permeated by the Orient but it is not pure and unadulterated like the foyers and vestibules. It is the European Byzantine Romanesque, which is the Orient as it came to us through the merchants of Venice, those great traders who brought the East and its art back to Europe in their minds, as they brought the cargoes in their ships."

"The Best Remaining Seats," Ben M. Hall, Clarkson N. Potter, Inc., New York.

Lamb leaned heavily on this column. It appeared first in Loew's State in Syracuse, later on 175th Street and 72nd Street in New York (see following pages) as did a number of other Hindu conceits off the same blueprints.

An extraordinary glass chandelier from the demolished Vanderbilt mansion found its way into the foyer of the Loew's State (1928) in Syracuse, New York.

Lamb's last great palaces are "permeated with a touch of the Orient—brightly colorful, emotional, and almost seductive" (*Motion Picture News*). The burnished bronze look of the Syracuse Loew's State (1928) was characterized by Lamb as "European Byzantine Romanesque, the Orient as it came to us through the merchants of Venice." Lamb was proudest of all of the grand foyer, "a temple of gold set with colored jewels."

The chandelier that originally hung in the foyer was another item the Loew's organization had salvaged from Vanderbilt's townhouse. The great central pendulum of stained glass was surrounded by smaller sconces with the same exotic bulbous form. Misguided concern during World War II that an enemy bombing of Syracuse might cause the chandelier to fall led to the fixture's removal. (It has since been sold in pieces, with orphaned sconces now on the living room walls of some American celebrities.)

Lamb hired Scottish craftsmen to do the theater's plasterwork ornament. The workers copied much of the design directly from scholarly works on Far Eastern architecure and art. The origin of the massive scrolled columns of the foyer can be directly traced to ancient columns from Hindu temples.

"American Picture Palaces," David Naylor, Van Nostrand Reinhold Co., New York.

Marquee Magazine, Fourth Quarter, 1994,
Theatre Historical Society of America, Elmhurst, Ill.

ISSN 0025-3928

Vol. 26 No. 4   THE JOURNAL OF THE THEATRE HISTORICAL SOCIETY OF AMERICA   FOURTH QUARTER 1994

The L-shaped double lobby is quite similar in layout and function to that in Loew's Midland, Kansas City. The outer leg (*far left*) sets the auditorium behind the office block while separating orchestra and balcony traffic. A small portion of the celebrated mural is visible on the right wall.

The inner portion (*above*) accesses the main floor and far side of the balcony. As in the Midland, the two areas are complementary in treatment but not identical.

Permutations of the mezzanine promenade (*left*) appeared in Loew's 72nd St. and 175th St., New York.

Another high tribute comes from performers. After praising the theater during a 1997 benefit there for Syracuse Stage, Gregory Peck inscribed this photo for auction at a fund-raiser.